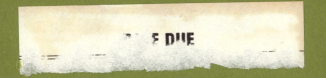

Metaphysics and Natural Philosophy

METAPHYSICS AND NATURAL PHILOSOPHY

The Problem of Substance in Classical Physics

P. M. Harman

Lecturer in History of Science,
University of Lancaster

THE HARVESTER PRESS · SUSSEX
BARNES & NOBLE BOOKS · NEW JERSEY

First published in Great Britain in 1982 by
THE HARVESTER PRESS LIMITED
Publisher: John Spiers
16 Ship Street, Brighton, Sussex

and in the USA by
BARNES & NOBLE BOOKS
81 Adams Drive, Totowa, New Jersey 07512

© P. M. Harman, 1982

British Library Cataloguing in Publication Data

Harman, P. M.
  Metaphysics and natural philosophy.
  1. Physics—Philosophy
  I. Title
  530'.01   QC6

  ISBN 0-7108-0451-2

Library of Congress Cataloging in Publication Data

Harman, P. M. (Peter Michael), 1943-
  Metaphysics and natural philosophy.
  Bibliography: p.
  Includes index.
  1. Physics—Philosophy. 2. Metaphysics. I. Title.
QC7.H26   530.1   82-4089
ISBN 0-389-20305-X   AACR2

Photoset in 11/12pt Baskerville by
Rowland Phototypesetting Limited
Bury St Edmunds, Suffolk
Printed in Great Britain by
The Thetford Press Limited
Thetford, Norfolk

To Timothy and Rosalind

Analytical table of contents

Chapter V   Faraday: the concept of the physical field   81

Chapter VI Helmholtz: the principle of the conservation of energy 105

Preface

The main aim of this study is to provide support for the thesis that the articulation of scientific theories rests on metaphysical as well as empirical constraints. Taking as its subject the conceptual structure of 'classical' (eighteenth- and nineteenth-century) physics, this book analyses the role of metaphysical arguments in justifying the conceptual foundations of scientific theories.

The traditional historiography of science has supposed that the 'scientific revolution' of the seventeenth century established the cognitive framework of subsequent science. 'Classical' physics is envisaged as philosophically monolithic and as synonymous with 'Newtonian' physics. By contrast, I will emphasise the conceptual diversity of the systems of physical theory comprising classical physics, and will highlight the role of metaphysics in the justification of the ontological assumptions of these physical theories. By focusing on some of the major concepts in the historical development of classical physics, concepts of force, inertia, energy and matter, I have aimed to provide an analysis of the status of the problem of substance and the associated concepts of force, energy, and the activity and passivity of matter in the physical theories of the eighteenth and nineteenth centuries. By an analysis of the role of metaphysical argument in justifying the ontological assumptions of physical theories, this book explores the conceptual foundations of classical physics.

In providing an analysis of the role of metaphysical foundations in the justification of the rationale of physical theories this study bears on problems in the epistemology of science. Both the instrumentalist view of science, that theories are symbolic representations which function as rules for the ordering of experience, and the empiricist interpretation of scientific realism, which justifies the reality of physical entities by appeal to empirical evidence, are inadequate as representations of the structure of theoretical discourses. By focusing on the role of metaphysical argument in science this study highlights the need to recognise the role of metaphysics as a constitutive part of scientific discourse.

During the time this book has taken shape I have learnt much from other scholars; their works are cited in the notes. An outline of the argument was presented to a conference on Newton held in Cambridge in 1977; and part of Chapter IV was presented to the International Conference on the History and Philosophy of Science in Montreal in 1980, and will be published in *Nature Mathematized* (Reidel), a volume of papers read at the conference. I am grateful for the interest expressed on these occasions. I have also drawn on some of my other writings, which provide detailed discussion of some special topics here more briefly treated.

I wish to express my gratitude to Gerd Buchdahl for stimulating and encouraging my work, and for our valuable discussions on Kant. I am grateful to J. E. McGuire, who first encouraged my work, especially for discussion of Newton's metaphysics and for our collaboration on eighteenth-century matter theory; to Charles Webster for his early and continued encouragement; and to D. T. Whiteside, especially for generously discussing the mathematical physics of Newton and his contemporaries. I also thank the Council of the Royal Society for the award of a grant for research undertaken during the preparation of this book.

CHAPTER I

Introduction

> The words 'attraction', 'impulse' or any 'propensity' to a centre, however, I employ indifferently and interchangeably, considering these forces not physically but merely mathematically. The reader should hence beware lest he think that by words of this sort I anywhere define a species or mode of action, or a physical cause or reason.[1]

With this disclaimer, strategically placed among the introductory definitions of his *Principia* (1687), Newton maintained that the concept of force was defined by the mathematical formalism of *Principia*, and that the laws of motion defined mathematical rather than physical, causal relations between material entities. Forces were relational, and Newton rejected the implication that he had grounded his 'mathematical principles of natural philosophy' on the physical existence and causal agency of forces. Following this assertion of the philosophical assumptions underlying Newton's mathematical physics, the development of 'classical' or 'Newtonian' physics in the eighteenth and nineteenth centuries is often characterised in terms of the emancipation from the concern with the essential nature of substances in favour of the symbolic representation of the mathematical relations between material entities.

Dijksterhuis described the philosophical framework of 'classical' physics in terms of the Newtonian 'mechanisation of the world picture', in which teleological explanations of natural phenomena were replaced by explanations in terms of mathematical, mechanical laws. According to this interpretation the problem of substance, concerned with the existential status of material reality, was resolved by the mathematical physics of Newton's mechanical theory of nature; it is claimed that 'substantial' thinking was replaced by the 'functional' mode of representation in 'classical' physics. Cassirer interpreted the mechanical models of 'classical' physics as heuristic analogies, viewing the articulation of physical models concerned with 'the existent as materially real' as being subordinated to the 'symbolism of principles'. The representation of the essential nature of substances was replaced by the elaboration of the 'functional' relations between material entities.[2]

In a classic study Meyerson emphasised that the representation of physical reality played an essential role in the explanatory framework of the theories of 'classical' physics, contesting Cassirer's interpretation which sought to explain the cognitive structure of 'classical' physics in terms of the abandonment of concern with the essential nature of material entities in favour of the expression of their mathematical relations. Meyerson maintained that the conceptual structure of 'classical' physics cannot be satisfactorily described in terms of the dominance of 'functional' over 'substantial' modes of representation, and that the ontological assumptions of 'classical' physics were integral to its articulation.[3] It is the aim of this book to explore the conceptual foundations of 'classical' physics by an analysis of the role of metaphysical argument in justifying the ontological assumptions of physical theories in the eighteenth and nineteenth centuries.

The problem can be described more precisely by referring to Cassirer's discussion of J. R. Mayer's theory of the conservation of 'force' of 1842, which Cassirer offered as an exemplification of his argument that functional representation became the dominant mode of theory construction in 'classical' physics. According to Cassirer, Mayer rejected any attempt to specify the ontological status of physical entities; Cassirer emphasised that for Mayer the conservation principle expressed 'an exact comparison between different things', representing the relation between different 'forces' such as heat and mechanical work.[4] Indeed, Mayer did emphasise that the causal relation between 'forces' only implied their indestructibility and transformability into one another, not the reducibility of one to the other. He affirmed that 'what heat, what electricity etc. are in their essence I do not know, as little as I know of the inner essence of a material substance'. As a result of his investigations he felt however that 'I see the connection of many phenomena much more clearly than has been seen hitherto', maintaining that the intelligibility of his concept of 'force' was grounded on his account of the connection between phenomena and the relations between 'forces'.

Despite this claim, Mayer's statement of the principle of the conservation of 'force' was grounded on the argument that 'force' was a substantial but nonmaterial entity and was conserved in a manner analogous to the conservation of matter. 'Forces are causes' he declared, so 'with them we may make full use of the principle: *causa aequat effectum* . . . this first property of all causes we call their indestructibility'. The conservation of 'force' was seen as an instance of the law of causality, the equivalence of causes and effects, exemplifying Meyerson's thesis that the quantitative equality of causes and effects implies their ontological status as substantial entities. Mayer asserted that 'to force as a cause corresponds force as an effect', and hence 'a force is no less indestructible than a substance'; he concluded that 'force' possessed the property of 'substantiality'. Nevertheless he emphasised that nature constituted a duality of matter and 'force', emphasising that the substantial nature of 'forces' did not grant them the status of material entities. 'Forces' were nonmaterial substances, and his claim of the conservation of 'forces' was based on the assertion of their ontological status as substantial entities.[5] Cassirer's stress on Mayer's statement of the 'functional' relations of 'forces' fails to comprehend Mayer's emphasis on their ontological status, ignoring the fundamental importance of the problem of substance in Mayer's theory of nature and the metaphysical argument employed by Mayer to establish the intelligibility of his theory of 'force'.[6]

By 'metaphysical' I mean the attempt to justify the conceptual rationale of a scientific theory by appeal to regulative maxims such as the law of causality or to criteria of simplicity, analogy or continuity; as well as to attempts to justify the intelligibility of a theory by an explication of the meaning of concepts of matter or force. As Buchdahl has emphasised, these 'metaphysical' arguments are intended to supplement the physical content of theories, based on the appeal to empirical confirmation and the systematic articulation of physical laws, purporting to provide grounds for the intelligibility of theories. By emphasising these 'metaphysical' components of scientific theories Buchdahl has stressed the interaction between the physical and metaphysical components in the articulation of scientific theories.[7]

In this study I shall emphasise that the enunciation of metaphysical foundations was a constitutive part of 'classical' physics, and will highlight the need for an explicit account of metaphysical foundations in any systematic account of the structure of scientific theories. As Kant declared in his *Metaphysical Foundations of Natural Science* (1786), 'all natural philosophers who wished to proceed mathematically' had been obliged to make 'use of metaphysical principles' to demonstrate the intelligibility of their conceptual assumptions,[8] and the aim of this study is to explain the role of metaphysical argument in the articulation of the natural philosophy of the eighteenth and nineteenth centuries.

The term 'natural philosophy' which was current in this period in denoting the science of physics is aptly descriptive, for the conceptual framework of 'classical' physics embraced metaphysical as well as physical components. In this book I am concerned to analyse a tradition of natural philosophy, a connected series of discourses whose articulation was in part shaped by the conceptual parameters of Newton's theory of nature. I do not however intend to imply that the history of physics in this period can be construed as a sequence of philosophical responses to conceptual tangles in an embracing 'Newtonian' tradition. The customary designation of eighteenth- and nineteenth-century physics as 'Newtonian' misleadingly conflates Newton's theory of nature and the physics of this later period, and ignores the conceptual diversity of eighteenth- and nineteenth-century physical theories and their significant departure from 'Newtonian' principles, as well as leaving out of account the important critiques of the philosophical framework of Newton's natural philosophy in the physical theories of the period. While the term 'classical' is appropriate when used to distinguish the philosophical assumptions of eighteenth- and nineteenth-century physics from the relativistic and indeterministic doctrines of twentieth-century or 'modern' physics, the term 'Newtonian' is misleading as a characterisation of the structure and content of eighteenth- and nineteenth-century physics.

Nevertheless, the status of the concept of substance in Newton's natural philosophy, and the relationship between Newton's laws of motion and concept of gravity and the metaphysical foundations of his natural philosophy, had an important bearing on subsequent debate in natural philosophy. While the mathematical facade of *Principia* presents a 'functional' mode of representation, Newton did attempt to formulate an ontology of forces. The ontological foundations of physical theory remained of fundamental importance in eighteenth- and nineteenth-century natural philosophy, and the definition of the concept of 'force' and its relation to Newton's theory of matter, and the relation between Newtonian physical laws and their metaphysical foundations, became the subject of important debate. Leibniz, Johann Bernoulli, Euler, Kant and others sought to analyse the concepts of force and matter, attempting to clarify the conceptual structure of natural philosophy and to explicate the relationship between physical laws and their metaphysical foundations. In the nineteenth century Helmholtz, Faraday and Maxwell reappraised the status of concepts of force and matter, formulating energy and field theories with explicit reference to ontological foundations and to the justification of their physical world views by appeal to metaphysical argument.

While these developments form a coherent tradition of natural philosophy, in that they form a set of historically and conceptually linked discourses whose articulation was in part shaped by the conceptual parameters of Newton's natural philosophy, their designation as 'Newtonian' would be totally misleading, as they were based on important critiques of the ontology and metaphysics of Newton's theory of nature. There were therefore significant rejections of Newton's physical theories and metaphysical arguments by eighteenth- and nineteenth-century natural philosophers. 'Classical' physics cannot be regarded as philosophically monolithic and as possessing a unified conceptual structure, but comprises a diversity of distinct natural philosophies which supposed ontologies containing physical entities in different mutual relations, and whose justification necessitated appeal to metaphysical argument.

By focusing on these debates on the metaphysical foundations of natural philosophy and by analysing their bearing on the development of energy and field theories, it is the aim of this book to study the metaphysical foundations and ontological assumptions of some of the systems of natural philosophy comprising 'classical' physics. In arguing that 'classical' physics comprises a diversity of distinct natural philosophies rather than constituting a unified conceptual system whose philosophical structure was established by 'Newtonian' physics, I shall contest the view, explicit in much historical writing on the 'scientific revolution' of the seventeenth century, that the metaphysical reorientation of thought which culminated in the Newtonian 'mechanisation of the world picture' established the cognitive framework and conceptual principles of eighteenth- and nineteenth-century science.[9] Despite the importance of the transformation in the cognitive structure of science associated with the seventeenth-century 'mechanisation of the world picture', and the impact of Newton's natural philosophy in establishing conceptual parameters which played a significant role in shaping the development of subsequent physical theory, the structure of natural philosophy in the eighteenth and nineteenth centuries cannot be represented as conforming to the principles of Newton's ontology and metaphysics.

In emphasising the ontological diversity of the systems of natural philosophy comprising the 'classical' physics of the eighteenth and nineteenth centuries, I shall highlight the close connection between new systems of physics and philosophical debates in this period. The development of these new systems of natural philosophy, and the consequent appeal to metaphysical argument as a means of justifying the intelligibility of these ontologies, provide examples of the function and nature of metaphysical argument in the articulation of scientific theories. In demonstrating that the reference to metaphysical foundations is constitutive of the conceptual development of 'classical' physics, this study aims to provide support for the thesis that the articulation of scientific theories rests on metaphysical as well as empirical constraints.

Notes

1 *Newton's Philosophiae Naturalis Principia Mathematica*, ed. A. Koyré and I. B. Cohen, 2 vols. (Cambridge, 1972), p. 46. Quoted from D. T. Whiteside's translation of the slightly variant draft in *The Mathematical Papers of Isaac Newton*, ed. D. T. Whiteside, Vol. 6 (Cambridge, 1974), p. 97.

2 E. J. Dijksterhuis, *The Mechanization of the World Picture*, trans. C. Dikshoorn (London, 1961), p. 501; E. Cassirer, *The Philosophy of Symbolic Forms. Volume Three: The Phenomenology of Knowledge* (London, 1957), pp. 459–68.

3 E. Meyerson, *Identity and Reality*, trans. K. Loewenberg (London, 1930), p. 388.

4 Cassirer, *Symbolic Forms*, Vol. 3, p. 462.

5 Quotations from J. R. Mayer, *Die Mechanik der Wärme*, ed. J. J. Weyrauch (Stuttgart, 1893), pp. 23, 31, 73, and *idem*, *Kleinere Schriften und Briefe*, ed. Weyrauch (Stuttgart, 1893), pp. 115, 180–1.

6 See P. M. Heimann, 'Mayer's concept of "force"', *Hist. Stud. Phys. Sci.*, 7 (1976), 277–96.

7 G. Buchdahl, 'History of science and criteria of choice', in *Historical and Philosophical Perspectives of Science*, ed. R. H. Stuewer (Minneapolis, 1970), pp. 204–30; *idem*, 'Neo-transcendental approaches towards scientific theory appraisal', in *Science, Belief and Behaviour*, ed. D. H. Mellor (Cambridge, 1980), pp. 1–21.

8 *Kants gesammelte Schriften*, Vol. 4 (Berlin, 1903), p. 472.

9 *Cf.* Dijksterhuis, *The Mechanization of the World Picture*; E. A. Burtt, *The Metaphysical Foundations of Modern Physical Science*, 2nd edn. (London, 1932); A. Koyré, *Newtonian Studies* (London, 1965).

CHAPTER II

Newton: force, inertia and the nature of matter

Law I. Every body perseveres in its state of resting or moving uniformly straight on, except inasmuch as it is compelled by impressed forces to change that state. . . .
Law II. Change in motion is proportional to the motive force impressed and takes place following the straight line along which that force is impressed. . . .
Law III. To any action there is always a contrary, equal reaction: in other words, the actions of two bodies each upon the other are always equal and opposite in direction.[1]

§1. Newton's mathematical principles of natural philosophy

The three 'axioms or laws of motion' which Newton placed among the introductory materials of his *Principia* (1687) have an important role in the conceptual structure of his natural philosphy. On the one hand the laws of motion provide a physical basis for the mathematical theory of motion expounded in the first two books of *Principia*; on the other, these laws ground Newton's theory of motion on the concept of 'force' and indicate the relationship between the concept of force and the nature of material substances.

Ontological issues were fundamental to the articulation of Newton's natural philosophy. While Newton maintained that the meaning of the concept of force was defined by the mathematical formalism of *Principia*, he did not remain content with a purely mathematical theory of force. Newton claimed to have established an experimental and mathematical natural philosophy, and disparaged metaphysical arguments, but the explanation of the causal agency of force led him to appeal to metaphysical and theological principles. In refusing to accept a natural philosophy grounded simply on principles of matter and motion, he affirmed a dualistic ontology of matter and force. The justification of his assumption of the essential passivity of matter, and the explication of the relation between matter and the forces which were the causes of the motions of bodies, were central problems in his natural philosophy, necessitating an appeal to metaphysical foundations.

These metaphysical issues arose directly from Newton's account of the physical basis of his theory of motion. Newton based his first law of motion on a relationship between 'force' as an external action generating change of motion and 'inertia' as a fundamental property of matter by which bodies resist changes in their state of rest or uniform rectilinear motion.[2] The status of force in Newton's natural philosophy was closely bound up with the ontological foundations of his theory of nature. Newton appealed to metaphysical arguments to justify his concept of inertia as an essential property of matter, and to demonstrate the intelligibility of his theory of the role of forces in nature.

An understanding of the status of the concept of force in Newton's natural philosophy requires some prior analysis of the principles of his mathematical theory of motion. In *Principia* Newton declares that the first two books of his treatise are not 'philosophical but merely mathematical': 'we are here concerned with mathematics'. He affirms that he is not concerned with the 'species of forces and their physical qualities', but with their 'quantities and mathematical proportions', and he makes it clear that he considers 'forces not physically but merely mathematically'. The concept of force was therefore defined by the mathematical formalism of *Principia* and did not imply a 'physical cause or reason' for the motions of bodies.[3] The use of terms such as 'attraction' and 'impulse' in describing the operation of forces had clear physical implications which, however, Newton wished to separate from the mathematical context which defined their function.

The major theme of Newton's *Principia* is the elaboration of a mathematical theory of the motions of bodies, especially the analysis of motion in time under the attraction of a central force. In the first theorem of *Principia* Newton demonstrates that the orbit of a body under the action of a central force could be represented by an infinite number of infinitesimal line-segments. He breaks down the action of a continuous force into a number of discrete impulses of force, each of equal magnitude; and the orbital arc traversed by the body under the action of the central force is split into a large number of line-segments, each traversed in equal times. By its 'inertia' (and according to the first law of motion) the body would tend to move in a straight line along the prolongation of each line-segment. But given the assumption that the action of a continuous force can be represented by a sequence of force impulses, by acting successively in a sequence of 'single but mighty' impulses the force would deflect the body along a succession of line-segments.[4] Thus a continuous force is measured by the effect it has in inducing a body to deviate from its rectilinear path, according to the second law of motion (which states that change of motion is proportional to the impressed force).

The mathematical argument is therefore fundamental to Newton's concept of force in *Principia*, and to the status of the laws of motion within the conceptual framework of Newton's natural philosophy. Newton's theory of planetary motion is based on the principle that a continuous force could be conceived as being broken down into an infinite number of component force impulses, each of which is infinitesimally small and acts instantaneously at successive infinitesimal instants of time, giving the resultant effect of continuous curvilinear motion.[5] In explaining his second law of motion in *Principia* Newton declares that a force generating motion could be 'impressed once and instantaneously or successively and gradually'.[6] In generating motion force would either act as a single impulse or (as in the case of a continuous force such as the attractive force of gravity) by the gradual and cumulative effect of an infinite number of discrete, infinitesimal force impulses. The concept of a continuous force as being represented by a succession of discrete force impulses is fundamental to Newton's mathematical theory of motion in *Principia*, and to the meaning and function of the second law of motion in Newton's 'mathematical principles of natural philosophy'.

In discussing his concept of a central force of attraction, which he terms 'centripetal' force in *Principia*, Newton observes that in calling centripetal forces 'attractions' he has used 'familiar' language; the concern in *Principia* was to establish a mathematical theory of motion, a quantitative measure rather than a conceptual explication of the nature of 'force'. Nevertheless he adds that the concept of centripetal force had physical implications, and that in the language of 'physics' centripetal forces should be termed 'impulses'.[7] While clearly separating the mathematical and physical levels of his argument, Newton does provide a physical interpretation of his concept of a continuous, centripetal attractive force of gravity. By basing centripetal force on the concept of impulsive forces, a physical argument which is grounded in his mathematical theory of the motion of a body under the action of a central force, Newton establishes his physics of motion as a generalisation of the physics of contact action and collision which had formed the core of seventeenth-century studies of mechanics, especially in the work of Descartes.[8] Newton's interpretation of force as a physical concept was based on his transformation of Descartes' theory of the motion and collision of bodies.

§2. The development of Newton's laws of motion

In 1664 Newton began a detailed study of Descartes' *Principles of Philosophy* (1664), paying careful attention to Descartes' statement of the 'laws of motion'. The first of these Cartesian 'rules' of motion states that 'every thing . . . continues to be in the same state, inasmuch as it is in it to do so [*quantum in se est*], and never changes except by external causes'. The second law of motion states that 'every part of matter, considered by itself, never tends to move along oblique lines, but only along straight lines'.[9] Descartes' phrase *quantum in se est* is significant in that it was later employed by Newton in *Principia*, and conveys the sense of a body moving 'naturally'.[10] Newton's reformulation of Descartes' first two laws of motion formed the basis of the first law of motion of *Principia*.

Descartes' third law of motion is concerned with the collision of bodies: 'if a body which moves and encounters another has less force to continue to move in a straight line than the other has to resist it, then it will be reflected in the other direction . . . if however it has more force, it moves the other body with it, and loses as much of its motion as it gives to it'. In this law Descartes asserts the conservation of 'motion' in collisions, the effect of collision on the motion of bodies being determined by calculating 'how much force there is in each body to move or to resist motion', and employing the principle that a stronger force will prevail over a weaker force. The application of this law of the conservation of 'motion' in determining how bodies change their motion in collisions depends on the measure of 'force'; and Descartes asserts that 'force' is estimated partly from the size of a body and partly from the body's speed of motion.[11] 'Force' is conceived as the causal principle maintaining a body in a state of motion, and changes in speed are caused by the opposition or contest of unequal forces.

Newton transformed this third Cartesian law of motion into the law of conservation of momentum, defining the conserved 'motion' (momentum) of a body in terms of the quantity of matter in a body (mass) and its velocity, emphasising the direction of motion, not merely (as with Descartes) the speed.[12]

Newton's development of the laws of motion in *Principia* was grounded on his transformation of Descartes' mechanics, and the concept of force is central to Newton's theory of motion. In expounding his laws of motion Descartes explains the tendency of a body to persevere in a state of rest or a state of motion in terms of the 'force' of a body to remain at rest and its 'force' to remain in a state of motion. He maintains that bodies have forces to act or resist motion because of his first law of motion, that every body tends, by its own nature, to remain in the same state. Hence, if a body is in motion it has a force to persevere in its state of motion; if it is at rest it has a force to persevere in its state of rest. Rest and motion are conceived as different states of a body, and it is a consequence of the first law of motion that a body, whether at rest or in motion, has a force continually maintaining the body in its state of rest or motion. In Descartes' physics force is the cause which maintains the existence of a body in any particular state, whether of rest or of motion. While Descartes maintains that extension constitutes the essence of body, he nevertheless affirms that the possession of a force, whether of rest or motion, is a necessary condition of the existence of bodies. When a body ceases to be in motion it is deprived of its force of motion; but the body at rest possesses a force of rest.[13]

§3. Force and inertia in Newton's physics

The key feature of Newton's development of Descartes' theory of motion is his special emphasis on the status of the concept of force in mechanics. In a draft treatise 'On the gravity and equilibrium of fluids', dating from about 1668, Newton expounded the Cartesian concept of force as the cause determining the state of rest or motion of a body:

> Force is the causal principle of motion and rest, and is either something external which, impressed in a certain body, either generates or destroys its motion, or at least to some extent changes it; or it is the internal principle by which the motion or rest imprinted on the body is conserved, and by which every entity endeavours to persevere in its actual state, and opposes itself to any impediment.

However Newton adds that 'inertia is the internal force of a body [ensuring] that its state is not easily changed by any external force'.[14] As Newton was aware, the term 'inertia' had been employed by Descartes to denote the tendency of bodies to assume a state of rest rather than a state of motion.[15] In a manner contrary to Descartes' usage, Newton here employs the term inertia to denote the force by which a body tends to persevere in its state of rest or motion. Newton considers the inertia of a body to be the property of a body to remain in the same state and to resist change by external causes. For Newton, Descartes' first law of motion is therefore to be explicated in terms of a fundamental property of matter, 'inertia', defined as an 'internal force' of a body.

The special status of inertia as an essential property of material substance is central to Newton's natural philosophy, and the relationship between the concepts of force and inertia is a crucial problem in his theory of nature. In *Principia* Newton transformed these concepts of force and inertia, but several strands of his earlier argument remained in his mature theory of motion. In 1684–5 he wrote a series of draft treatises 'On the motion of bodies', material which culminated in the published *Principia* (1687). His successive drafts of definitions of force and inertia shed light on the evolution of his ideas, and on the conceptual status of inertia, and its relation to his theory of substance, in his mature natural philosophy. In the early versions of his definitions Newton adheres to his earlier (and Cartesian) conception of force as the principle maintaining a body in a state of rest or motion. He defines the 'innate, inherent and essential force [*vis insita innata et essentialis*] of a body' as the 'power by which it perseveres in its state of resting or of moving uniformly in a straight line', referring to the force by which a body endeavours to preserve its motion as the 'force of motion' of the body.[16]

Newton however abandoned this explication of the force of motion of a body, distinguishing between the power by which a body perseveres in a state of rest or uniform rectilinear motion (inertia) and the impressed force which acts to bring about a change of motion. Drawing on his earlier use of the concept of inertia to denote the internal force by which a body persisted in its state of rest or motion, in a draft (preserved in the published text of *Principia*) he defines the 'innate force' or 'inertia' of matter as the 'power of resisting whereby each individual body, inasmuch as it is in it to do so [*quantum in se est*], perseveres in its state of resting or of moving uniformly straight on'. In the published text Newton added the further definitional clarification: 'the innate force may be called, by a very significant name, the force of inertia [*vis inertiae*]'. The concept of the 'force' of 'inertia' thus denotes the internal power of matter ('innate force') by which a body persists in its state of rest or uniform rectilinear motion.

Newton then provides a new definition of the concept of force. In a draft (again preserved in the published text of *Principa*) Newton defines the force of motion of a body as the 'impressed force', the 'action exerted on a body to change its state either of resting still or moving uniformly straight on'. Newton emphasises that the force of motion ('impressed force') is not internal to the material substance of the body. He declares that 'impressed force' consists in 'action alone, and does not endure in the body after the action is over'. In the published text Newton added the further clarification: 'a body perseveres in every new state by the force of inertia alone', not by the 'impressed force' remaining in a body after the action of that 'impressed force' has ceased. In a later (unpublished) annotation he observed that 'impressed force' is 'not essential to body', emphasising the distinction between 'impressed force' and 'inertia'.[17]

In *Principia* Newton thus rejects the notion that the force of motion of a body could be construed as an 'internal principle' by which motion or rest is preserved in bodies. The disjunction between the concepts of 'impressed force' and 'inertia' expresses the distinction between 'external' causes generating changes in the state of rest or motion of a body, and the internal, inherent power (inertia) by which bodies resist the action of an external impressed force. These new concepts of impressed force and inertia provided the explanatory framework for the first law of motion of *Principia*, that 'every body perseveres in its state of resting or moving uniformly straight on, except inasmuch as it is compelled by impressed forces to change that state'.

While Newton clearly differentiates this concept of force as an action externally impressed upon a body from the concept of inertia which denotes an internal power persisting in material substances, his designation of the concept of inertia as the 'force of inertia [*vis inertiae*]' is ambiguous. As Euler observed in an essay 'On the origin of forces' (1750), strictly speaking the concepts of 'force' and 'inertia' were 'directly contrary to one another'; while 'force' was the cause of a change of motion, 'inertia' preserved a body in a state of motion or rest.[18] Newton introduced the term *vis inertiae* by analogy with *vis insita* ('innate force'), the inherent power of matter by which a body persists in its state of rest or uniform rectilinear motion, declaring that 'innate force' may be called 'force of inertia'. The term *vis insita* was not uncommon in the seventeenth century, meaning 'natural power' or 'inherent force', and Newton used this term to denote the 'natural' internal power by which a body resists any change of state 'inasmuch as it is in it to do so [*quantum in se est*]'.[19] Despite terminological ambiguities, Newton does not confuse inertia and impressed force in *Principia*.

The concept of inertia is therefore fundamental to the

intelligibility of Newton's first law of motion, providing an explanation of the 'natural' tendency of a body to persevere in the same state of rest or uniform rectilinear motion. Newton emphasises that inertia is 'proportional to bodily bulk', and he refers to the 'inertia' of the 'mass' of a body.[20] In the third rule of philosophising that Newton appended to the second edition of *Principia* (1713) he listed 'inertia' together with extension, hardness, impenetrability and mobility as the 'universal' qualities of matter, the essential properties an entity would have to possess as a necessary and sufficient condition of its materiality.[21] The possession of inertia was therefore one of the defining qualities of a material body. The concept of inertia, which explains a body's perseverance in its state of rest or uniform rectilinear motion, is therefore conceived as a defining property of material substances.

The clarification of the distinction between force and inertia was fundamental to Newton's theory of motion, and established the intelligibility of Newton's first law of motion (which is based on the concept of inertia conceived as a defining property of bodies), the role of the first law of motion being to establish the framework of Newton's mechanics and the relationship between force as an external action and inertia as an internal property of bodies. While Newton insisted that the meaning of the concept of force was defined by the mathematical formalism of *Principia* and that his account of the motions of bodies did not presuppose a physical explanation of the nature of force, the intelligibility of the concept of force is grounded on Newton's clarification of force and inertia as distinct mechanical concepts and hence on the enunciation of the relationship between impressed force as an external action producing change of motion and inertia as a fundamental property of matter by which bodies resist change of rest or motion.

Ontological issues were therefore fundamental to the development of Newton's natural philosophy, and the problem of substance is of crucial significance for the conceptual coherence of his theory of mechanics in *Principia*. The nature of matter and its relation to the forces which were the causes of the diverse motions of the particles of matter became for Newton a basic problem requiring analysis; and in seeking to justify the conceptual framework of his mechanics he appealed to metaphysical arguments, so as to explicate his assumption that inertia was an essential property of matter and to explain the causal role of forces in determining the structure of material reality.

§4. Newton's theory of matter and space

Newton had already elaborated some of the distinctive themes of his philosophy of matter in his draft treatise 'On the gravity and equilibrium of fluids.' (*c.* 1668), where he developed his metaphysics of nature in the context of a critique of Descartes' theory of matter. Newton rejected Descartes' concept of substance, that the occupancy of space was the essential attribute of matter. For Newton spatial extension is neither a substance nor an attribute of substance; he declares that 'it has its own manner of existence which fits neither substances nor accidents'. He argues that it is possible to imagine spaces empty of material substances and that 'we cannot believe that [space] would perish with the body if God should annihilate a body'. Newton therefore concludes that 'although space may be empty of body, nevertheless it is not in itself a void; and *something* is there, because spaces are there'. Newton maintains that space is an incorporeal physical entity which is independent of material bodies, and that space is the unconditioned condition for the existence of material entities.

The thrust of Newton's argument is to demolish the Cartesian theory of substance by maintaining that while 'extension is not created but has existed eternally', matter is a 'derivative and incomplete reality', and its existence is contingent on God's will. To grant matter a 'complete, absolute, independent reality' like space would 'manifestly offer a path to Atheism'; hence he asserts that matter cannot be defined as spatial extension. In contrast to the Cartesian concept of substance, Newton defines bodies as 'determined quantities of extension which omnipresent God endows with certain conditions', emphasising that matter must be characterised by the possession of other properties in addition to spatial extension.[22] In the years following the publication of *Principia* Newton elaborated a concept of substance which supposed that the possession of

inertia and other essential qualities, not simply spatial extension, defined the nature of material entities.

While Newton did not finally abandon the explanation of
planetary motion by the rotary action of vortices of matter until
the early 1680s,[23] his deep-rooted opposition to the Cartesian
theory of matter foreshadows his formulation in *Principia* of a
cosmology based on the action of centripetal attractive forces in
void space rather than the impact of particles constituting a
plenum, rejecting the Cartesian view that there could be no
space empty of matter since the occupancy of space was the
essential attribute of matter. In enunciating his theory of
matter Newton emphasises the perceptibility and tangibility of
matter, not simply its spatial extension, stressing that substance is 'an entity that can act upon things', a property that
could not be grounded on extension alone.[24]

§5. The essential properties of matter and the 'analogy of nature'

Newton consistently insists that his physics is grounded upon
experiment and experience and on the perceptible characteristics of bodies. In the 1717 *Opticks* he declares that 'the main
business of natural philosophy is to argue from phenomena
without feigning hypotheses'. By 'phenomena', as he made
clear in various draft definitions dating from 1715–16, he
meant 'whatever things [that] can be perceived'. He maintains
that 'phenomena' are the objects of physical inquiry: 'what are
not phenomena, and subject to none of the senses, have no
place in experimental philosophy'. This forthright definition of
the scope of physics raised difficulties for Newton's ontology,
for he did not maintain that all the physical bodies in the
universe were perceptible and subject to experimental investigation. The assumption that bodies were composed of
imperceptible atoms was a fundamental assumption of his
theory of nature, and in a famous statement in the *Opticks* he
declared that these 'primitive particles' were 'solid, massy,
hard, impenetrable, moveable particles'.[25]

Despite this affirmation of the essential properties characterising the primordial atoms he denies that the primordial
particles in nature are observable. He emphasises that the

smallest particles composing bodies reflect very little light and hence will appear black because light is 'reflected and refracted within them until it be stifled and lost'. Hence the primordial particles are imperceptible: 'it seems impossible to see the more secret and noble works of nature'.[26] Given Newton's emphasis on the grounding of all knowledge of physical bodies on perceivable phenomena, the primordial atoms have a questionable status in his theory of physics. This problem posed acute difficulties for Newton, for he was convinced that it was impossible to conceive physical entities which were not characterised by properties such as impenetrability and hardness; and this theory of the essential properties of matter and his ontology of atoms and void space highlighted his renunciation of the Cartesian theory of substance.

The justification of the hardness and impenetrability of the ultimate particles in nature was in question, because any statement of the intrinsic properties of imperceptible bodies must go beyond the evidence of the senses. It was to meet this difficulty that Newton began, in the 1690s, to draft philosophical arguments which culminated in the third of the rules of philosophising that he included in the prefatory section of the third book of the second edition of *Principia* (1713). In the first of these drafts Newton appeals to the 'analogy of nature' to justify the assumption that 'the laws of all bodies in which experiments can be made are the laws of bodies universally'. As he emphasised later, 'without [the third rule of philosophising] we cannot affirm that all bodies are impenetrable'. By means of analogical argument Newton wished to establish the properties of the imperceptible, primordial particles, basing the ascription of properties of the unobservable atoms on the perceptible characteristics of the phenomenal bodies which become 'known only by means of the senses'.[27]

Newton's appeal to analogical argument here poses acute difficulties to his avowedly empiricist philosophy. Assertions about the invisible realm of primordial atoms could not in principle be tested directly against the evidence of the senses, because the primordial corpuscles are (Newton declares) unobservable. In drafts clearly directed against Leibniz's theory of substance, which denied that the observable properties of bodies such as extension and impenetrability constitute the defining characteristics of matter, he declared: 'things which cannot be perceived, but yet are hypothetically termed bodies by some people, these things are more properly treated of in metaphysics'.[28] By the standard of his own categories Newton's theory of matter was metaphysical, even though the appeal to experiment and experience served to conceal the metaphysical basis of Newton's analogical argument. While Newton's purpose in stating the third rule of philosophising was to emphasise the plausibility of applying the laws of motion of *Principia* to the mechanics of unobservable particles rather than to enunciate a philosophy of matter, this rule was of fundamental importance in justifying the universality of Newton's mechanics to all bodies in nature. Newton's argument in the third rule of philosophising is therefore of central importance to an understanding of the metaphysical foundations of Newton's mechanics.

In the third rule of philosophising Newton states that 'the qualities of bodies which cannot be intended and remitted [of degrees], and which apply to all bodies in which experiments can be made, are qualities of all bodies universally'. Newton declares that these universal qualities are those of 'extension, hardness, impenetrability, mobility and inertia [*vis inertiae*]', and argues that these properties are known through experience. He justifies the ascription of these qualities to the imperceptible 'indivisible particles' of bodies by appeal to the 'analogy of nature', and declares that the ascription of these qualities to all bodies in nature is the 'foundation of all philosophy'.[29]

The 'universal' qualities of matter were therefore essential to the materiality of entities; and in a draft of the rule Newton contrasts these universal qualities with qualities such as 'heat and cold, wet and dry, light and darkness, colour and blackness', invoking the distinction between primary and secondary qualities employed by seventeenth-century philosophers to distinguish intrinsic properties of substances which exist independently of human perception, from properties which were held to arise as a result of a relation between the perceiving mind and the primary qualities of matter which provided their causal nexus. Newton grounds this distinction on the argument that the 'universal' qualities such as extension and impenetrability do not intend and remit of degrees; these qualities are held not to manifest continuous and successive gradations of intensity. He explains the principle more fully in a draft: 'a quality which cannot be remitted cannot be taken away . . . that which can be taken away, if it were to be taken away from some parts of the whole, it could be remitted in the whole'.[30]

Newton's terminology is drawn from medieval philosophy, and he employed this argument so as to define the 'universal' qualities which were essential to matter and could not change without affecting the materiality of an entity, and to distinguish these 'universal' qualities from the properties of matter which could change without affecting the status of matter *qua* substance. The 'universal' qualities define the necessary and sufficient conditions of the materiality of bodies, and Newton believed that his criterion of intension and remission of degrees could adequately distinguish between the essential qualities of matter and those properties which could manifest varying degrees of intensity without affecting the materiality of bodies. He justifies the ascription of the essential qualities to the imperceptible particles of matter by appealing to the uniformity and homogeneity of nature, referring to the 'analogy of nature' and to the argument that nature is 'simple and always consonant to itself'.[31] Hence the primordial atoms differ only in size, not in their essential properties, from observable particles; nature is unified by the doctrine of essential qualities as stated in the third rule of philosophising.

The third rule of philosophising offers a definition of matter which contrasts markedly with Descartes' concept of extension as constituting the essence of body, a doctrine which Newton had disparaged in the 1660s. In particular, the concept of inertia, which was crucial to the conceptual framework of the theory of motion in *Principia*, is declared to be one of the defining properties of matter. The third rule serves to justify the intelligibility of Newton's mechanics, by demonstrating the fundamental conceptual status of inertia as one of the 'natural real reasonable manifest qualities of all bodies seated in them by the will of God',[32] and hence to establish the concept of inertia as a universal property of matter by which bodies resist change. Just as Newton's transformation of Descartes' theory of motion led to the enunciation in *Principia* of a mechanics grounded on the disjunction between the concepts of force and inertia, in enunciating a theory of matter which would re-appraise the ontological assumptions of the Cartesian mech-anical philosophy Newton demonstrated the fundamental status of the concept of inertia as a defining property of matter.

§6. The explanation of the force of gravity

In *Principia* Newton makes a distinction between mathematics which is concerned with the 'quantities and proportions' of forces, and physics which is concerned with the comparison between these mathematical proportions and physical phenom-ena; and he makes a further distinction between the discussion of physical reality and the problem of determining the 'causes' and 'species' of the forces.[33] This separation of the different levels of explanation in natural philosophy is fundamental to the strategy of *Principia*, but Newton clearly envisages that the explanation of the causal role of forces is a central issue in natural philosophy even though this problem is excluded from consideration in his treatise on the mathematical principles of motion and their application to the physical world. In the years following the publication of *Principia* Newton devoted consider-able attention to the explication of the causal role of forces in nature, and many of his arguments were published in the queries which were appended to the first Latin edition of the *Opticks* in 1706 and which were further developed in the second English edition published in 1717.

Newton's discussion of the nature of forces was bound up with his concern to explain the nature of the force of gravity, and he gave a famous statement of his views in a letter to the theologian Richard Bentley in 1693. Newton declared that it was 'unconceivable that inanimate brute matter should (with-out the mediation of something else which is not material) operate upon and affect other matter without mutual contact'. Hence he denied that 'gravity should be innate inherent and essential to matter so that one body may act upon another at a distance through a vacuum without the mediation of any thing else by and through which their action or force may be conveyed'. To suppose action at a distance was a philosophical 'absurdity'; but while Newton declared that 'gravity must be caused by an agent acting constantly according to certain laws', he declined to assert whether 'this agent be material or immaterial'.[34]

Newton thus affirmed his commitment that it was necessary to provide some form of causal explanation of gravity, though he here left open the question as to whether gravity was caused by the mediation of some form of material substance acting between planetary bodies, or by 'the mediation of something else which is not material'. To suppose that matter could act directly at a distance without the mediation of some agent would imply that gravity was 'innate inherent and essential to matter', that the causal explanation of gravity was to be found in the nature of material substances. Newton vehemently rejected this view. His use of the phrase 'innate inherent and essential' echoed his drafts of the definitions of *Principia*, where he had defined inertia as an 'innate, inherent and essential force' of a body.[35] As a force acting on planetary bodies gravity was in a different category to inertia; and Newton's strict distinction in *Principia* between forces acting to bring about change of motion and inertia as a 'universal' or 'essential' property of matter, a power by which bodies persisted in their state of motion or rest, implied that gravity was not an inherent or essential property of matter.

§7. Forces, active principles and ethers

Newton does however provide a clue about the kind of explanation he believed to be appropriate to explain the nature of gravity. He clearly distinguished between gravity and those physical properties—hardness, extension, inertia—that he held to be intrinsic to the nature of matter. In the *Opticks* Newton contrasts inertia as a 'passive principle by which bodies persist in their motion or rest' and which is 'accompanied with such passive laws of motion as naturally result from that force [of inertia]', with certain 'active principles, such as are the cause of gravity'.

This fundamental duality of active and passive principles reflects Newton's emphasis on the status of matter as a derivative entity whose existence and activity is contingent on God's will. To grant matter inherent powers of activity would be to allow matter to have the status of a self-sufficient entity, a doctrine which for Newton was tantamount to atheism. He emphasises that matter in itself does not have the capacity to sustain motion and the active powers of the cosmos. Passive principles such as inertia, which explains the power of bodies to persist in their state of rest or motion, could not explain the origin of motion in the world. Moreover, because motion is constantly being dissipated, in the collision of inelastic or partially elastic bodies for example, it was apparent that 'some other principle is necessary for conserving the motion'. Thus he declares that 'the variety of motion which we find in the world is always decreasing, [and hence] there is a necessity of conserving it and recruiting it by active principles'. The motion and activity of bodies in nature is therefore seen in terms of the causal agency of 'active principles'.[36]

The concept of 'active principles' is therefore fundamental to the conceptual rationale of Newton's theory of gravity. As his argument makes clear, the problem of the cause of gravity necessitated appeal to metaphysical argument. The deficiency of the concept of action at a distance required the enunciation of a causal explanation; and to avoid the inference that gravity was an innate property of matter, Newton locates the explanation of gravity in terms of the agency of 'active principles' whose operation is held to be distinct from the 'passive' laws of matter. As he emphasises in a draft, these active principles are 'much more potent than are the passive laws of motion arising from the Vis inertiae of the matter'.[37] The exact status of 'active principles' remained unclear in the published queries, where Newton refers to active principles as being both the 'cause of gravity' and as being 'general laws of nature . . . such as is that of gravity'. This ambiguity is clarified in his drafts, where he refers to God as the cause of the 'force of gravity' by 'the mediation of some active principle'.[38]

Active principles therefore functioned both as laws of nature (though not 'passive' laws of matter) and as the mediating agents by which God conserved motion and gravity in the cosmos, being regarded as the manifestation of God's lawful, causal agency in nature. For Newton, the intelligibility of the concept of gravity is established by appeal to a physico-theological argument.

In conceiving active principles as manifest in laws of nature

Newton maintained a disjunction between active principles and the will of God; and in stressing the distinction between active and passive principles he made it clear that the operations of active principles within the natural order were not reducible to the passive principles of matter. In the published queries he links the agency of active principles to chemical phenomena, seeking to establish the operation of active principles as natural agents whose mode of action was distinct from the 'passive' laws of *Principia*. Referring to a diversity of 'great and violent' chemical processes he asserted that in these processes the particles of bodies 'are put into new motions by a very potent principle'. In a draft he expressed the point with strong emphasis: 'the above mentioned motions are so great & violent as to shew that (in Fermentations) there is new motion in the world generated from other Principles than the usual laws of motion' which arise from inertia and the passive principles of matter.[39]

These passages attest to his concern to affirm that while active principles were the manifestation of God's causal agency in nature they were also natural agents; and that as the mediating agents by which God sustained the force of gravity these active principles could not be interpreted as inherent properties of matter. The thrust of Newton's argument was to emphasise that while the distance force of gravity was a natural agent operating constantly according to the mathematical law of gravity, gravity itself was not an essential property of matter. The appeal to active principles was intended to establish the intelligibility of the phenomenon of gravity.

In these passages Newton envisaged chemical change as a type of living process, and in a draft he declared that 'we cannot say that all nature is not alive'.[40] The appeal to vivifying principles is a constant theme in Newton's natural philosophy. In his 'Hypothesis explaining the properties of light' (1675) he had conjectured that 'the whole frame of nature may be nothing but aether condensed by a fermental principle'. He suggested that nature 'may be nothing but various con-textures of some certaine aethereall spirits or vapours', speculating that 'perhaps may all things be originated from aether'. Newton added that 'nature is a perpetuall circulatory worker', and he conjectured that by the chemical transformations of ethereal spirits and by 'nature making a circulation' the activity of the cosmos could be conserved.[41] In appealing to chemical, active ethereal spirits Newton evoked an alchemical cosmology.[42] Using terms analogous to his theory of active principles, this ethereal cosmology lay outside the framework of the passive laws of matter and motion.

Newton's discussion of active principles as the cause of gravity highlighted a crucial feature of his natural philosophy, his refusal either to espouse an explanation of gravity based on the appeal to a plenum of material vortices, or to countenance the suggestion that attraction was an inherent property of matter. In introducing the disjunction between the passive principles of matter and active principles as the cause of gravity Newton emphasised, in the *Opticks*, that he did not suppose these active principles to be 'occult qualities', constitutive properties of matter.[43]

These issues were raised by Leibniz, questioning the conceptual framework of Newton's natural philosophy. In a letter to Newton in 1693 Leibniz applauded Newton's ability to 'handle nature in mathematical terms' but expressed his belief that gravity was 'caused or regulated by the motion of a fluid medium'.[44] In a discussion in 1711, clearly aimed at Newton, Leibniz declared that any theory of gravity which supposed 'that the thing is performed without any mechanism' or 'by a law of God' would suppose gravity to be 'an unreasonable occult quality'.[45] Newton's response was characteristically pungent, though it remained unpublished, refusing to accept Leibniz's premise that a physical explanation of gravity must be explicated in terms of a contact-action model of matter in motion. Newton rejects the suggestion that if an explanation was not 'mechanical' it must be a 'miracle', an 'occult quality' and a 'fiction'. Nevertheless Newton had not provided a physical illustration of the agency of active principles, other than associating these active principles with chemical phenomena and emphasising that they could not be subsumed under a mechanism of matter in motion. He went on to suggest that gravity could be caused 'by a power seated in a substance in wch bodies move & flote without resistance & wch therefore has no vis inertiae but acts by other laws than those that are mechanical.'[46]

In this remarkable statement Newton is envisaging the explanation of gravity by a substance which did not possess the passivity and inertia of ordinary matter but was, by implication, an 'active principle'. This speculation probably shaped his reference to a 'subtle spirit' in the General Scholium to the second edition of *Principia* (1713), which he qualifies as an 'electric and elastic' spirit in a marginal note in his own copy of *Principia*.[47] In this period electricity rather than chemistry seemed to Newton to be the key to the agency of active principles, and in drafts he speculated that 'all bodies therefore abound with a very subtile, but active, potent, electric spirit', which he referred to as a 'subtile Aether or Aetherial elastic spirit'.[48]

Newton therefore returned to the concept of the ether to provide a physical model for the operation of active principles, for the ether of his 1675 'Hypothesis on light' served the same function as the active principles of the *Opticks* in purporting to explain the activity of nature. These speculations culminated in his introduction of an ether in the queries to the 1717 *Opticks* to explain optical reflection and refraction and to provide a causal explanation for gravity. Newton argues that

> the exceeding smallness of its particles may contribute to the greatness of the force by which those particles may recede from one another, and thereby make that medium exceedingly more rare and elastic than air, and by consequence exceedingly less able to resist the motions of projectiles, and exceedingly more able to press upon gross bodies, by endeavouring to expand it self.[49]

In suggesting this theory to explain the agency of gravity Newton is not invoking the Cartesian concept of the impact of particles constituting a plenum. In the General Scholium to the second edition of *Principia* he had argued that 'gravity must proceed from a cause that penetrates to the very centres of the sun and planets' and that 'operates not according to the quantity of the surface of the particles upon which it acts (as mechanical causes are accustomed)'.[50] In referring to the pressing of the ether particles Newton is not suggesting the Cartesian 'mechanical' model of the impact of particles. Nor is he envisaging a medium acting by fluid pressure, for as he pointed out in the *Opticks*, at any point in a fluid the pressure

acts equally in all directions, whereas 'gravity tends down-
wards'.[51] Hence fluid pressure cannot explain the directionality
of gravity. Newton emphasises that gravity cannot be reduced
to 'mechanical' or contact-action theories.

Newton envisages the ether acting by a differential density
arising from the repulsive force exerted by its minute particles.
The great 'elastick force' of the ether, its tendency to 'expand it
self', enabled it to 'press upon gross bodies' and hence to cause
planets to approach or recede. Newton claims that just as the
small size of light corpuscles implied forces of great intensity in
relation to size, the particles of ether, which were 'exceedingly
smaller than those of air, or even than those of light', were
endowed with the strongest forces with respect to their minute
size. Ether was composed of 'particles which endeavour to
recede from one another', its particles being separated by void
space and acting on one another by their repulsive forces. The
agency of the ether was manifested through the differential
density of the ethereal 'medium'.[52]

In rejecting the reducibility of gravity to a contact-action
model of the impact of particles, Newton conceives the ether of
the 1717 *Opticks* as an active principle communicating God's
lawful, causal agency and as a physical model (though not a
contact-action model) establishing the intelligibility of the
distance force of gravity. In distinguishing between the inertia
and passivity of ordinary matter and the active properties of
ether, and in stressing the difference between his ether model
and the Cartesian contact-action plenum, Newton provides a
physical representation of the agency of active principles, and
hence an explication of the coherence of his theory of gravity.[53]

Despite Newton's disjunction between the passivity of
ordinary matter and the activity of the ether, the ether has an
ambiguous conceptual status in his natural philosophy. Composed of particles of matter, ether would ostensibly appear to
fall under the category of passive principles, and his use of ether
as an active principle threatened the active-passive dualism of
his natural philosophy. Similarly, his use of the term 'force of
inertia' is ambiguous, blurring his clear conceptual distinction
between inertia as a passive property of matter and force as an
external action generating change. These issues were to be
discussed by subsequent natural philosophers, seeking in

Newton's writings a consistent account of the metaphysical assumptions—about the nature of matter and force, and the status of the concept of gravitational attraction—underlying his mathematical theory of the motions of terrestrial and celestial bodies, and his physical principles of motion as stated in the laws of motion of *Principia*.

In seeking to provide conceptual foundations for his physical theories, Newton formulated an ontology of force and substance. In grounding his theory of motion on the concept of inertia, Newton appealed to metaphysical argument in his third rule of philosophising to establish inertia as an essential property of material substances. To explicate his theory of gravity he appealed to a physico-theological argument, enunciating a distinction between active principles and the passive principles of matter. Newton's appeal to metaphysical argument exemplifies the role of metaphysics in the justification of physical theories and the relationship between substantial and functional representation in Newtonian natural philosophy.

Notes

1 *Newton's Philosophiae Naturalis Principia Mathematica*, ed. A. Koyré and I. B. Cohen, 2 vols. (Cambridge, 1972), pp. 54–5. Translation quoted from *The Mathematical Papers of Isaac Newton*, ed. D. T. Whiteside, Vol. 6 (Cambridge, 1974), pp. 97–9.

2 Newton, *Principia*, pp. 40–1.

3 Newton, *Principia*, pp. 549, 266, 298, 46.

4 Newton, *Principia*, pp. 88–9. For further analysis see Whiteside, ed., *Mathematical Papers*, Vol. 6, pp. 35–7, and *idem*, 'The mathematical principles underlying Newton's *Principia Mathematica*', *J. Hist. Astron.*, 1 (1970), 116–38.

5 For further discussion see Whiteside, ed., *Mathematical Papers*, Vol. 6, pp. 540–1.

6 Newton, *Principia*, p. 54; Whiteside, ed., *Mathematical Papers*, Vol. 6, p. 98.

7 Newton, *Principia*, p. 266. On Newton's introduction of the concept of 'centripetal' force see D. T. Whiteside, 'Before the *Principia*', *J. Hist. Astron.*, 1 (1970), 5–19.

8 *Cf.* I. B. Cohen, *The Newtonian Revolution* (Cambridge, 1980), p. 176.

9 *Oeuvres de Descartes*, ed. C. Adam and P. Tannery, 13 vols. (Paris, 1897–1913), Vol. 8, part i, pp. 62–4.

10 *Cf.* Newton's rendering of Descartes' first law of motion in 1665. See J. W. Herivel, *The Background to Newton's 'Principia'* (Oxford, 1965), p. 153. See

also I. B. Cohen, '*Quantum in se est*: Newton's concept of inertia in relation to Descartes and Lucretius', *Notes and Records*, 19 (1964), 131–55.

[11] Descartes, *Oeuvres*, Vol. 8–i, pp. 65–7. See also A. Gabbey, 'Force and inertia in the seventeenth century: Descartes and Newton', in *Descartes: Philosophy, Mathematics and Physics*, ed. S. Gaukroger (Brighton, 1980), pp. 230–320.

[12] Herivel, *Background*, p. 142.

[13] Descartes, *Oeuvres*, Vol. 8–i, p. 66. See also M. Gueroult, 'Métaphysique et physique de la force chez Descartes', *Etudes sur Descartes, Spinoza, Malebranche et Leibniz* (Hildesheim, 1970), pp. 85–121 (trans. in Gaukroger, *Descartes*, pp. 196–229).

[14] Herivel, *Background*, p. 231.

[15] Cohen, *Newtonian Revolution*, pp. 189, 333–4.

[16] Whiteside, ed., *Mathematical Papers*, Vol. 6, p. 191. See also Gabbey, 'Force and inertia', pp. 272–9.

[17] Whiteside, ed., *Mathematical Papers*, Vol. 6, pp. 93–5; Newton, *Principia*, pp. 40–1.

[18] L. Euler, 'Recherches sur l'origine des forces', *Opera Omnia*, series II, Vol. 5, ed. J. O. Fleckenstein (Lausanne, 1957), p. 112. *Cf.* R. S. Westfall, *Force in Newton's Physics* (London, 1971) pp. 448–56, and E. McMullin, *Newton on Matter and Activity* (London, 1978), pp. 33–43.

[19] Cohen, *Newtonian Revolution*, pp. 191, 334.

[20] Newton, *Principia*, p. 40.

[21] Newton, *Principia*, p. 552.

[22] 'De gravitatione et aequipondio fluidorum', *Unpublished Scientific Papers of Isaac Newton*, ed. A. R. Hall and M. Boas Hall (Cambridge, 1962), pp. 132–44. See J. E. McGuire, 'Body and void and Newton's *De Mundi Systemate*', *Arch. Hist. Exact Sci.*, 3 (1966), 206–48.

[23] Whiteside, 'Before the *Principia*'.

[24] *Unpublished Scientific Papers*, p. 132; Descartes, *Oeuvres*, Vol. 8–i, p. 45.

[25] Isaac Newton, *Opticks*, 4th edn. (London, 1952), pp. 369, 400. Newton MSS trans. in McGuire, 'Body and void', pp. 220–1, 238.

[26] Newton, *Opticks*, pp. 262, 340. *Cf.* J. E. McGuire, 'Atoms and the "analogy of nature": Newton's third rule of philosophizing', *Stud. Hist. Phil. Sci.*, 1 (1970), 3–57.

[27] Newton MSS quoted in J. E. McGuire, 'The origin of Newton's doctrine of essential qualities', *Centaurus*, 12 (1968), 236, and A. Koyré and I. B. Cohen, 'Newton and the Leibniz-Clarke correspondence', *Arch. Int. d'Hist. Sci.*, 15 (1962), 113.

[28] Newton MS trans. in McGuire, 'Body and void', p. 221.

[29] Newton, *Principia*, pp. 552–4.

[30] Newton MS trans. in McGuire, 'Newton's doctrine of essential qualities', p. 237.

[31] Newton, *Principia*, p. 553. *Cf.* McGuire, 'Atoms and the "analogy of nature"' and McMullin, *Newton on Matter*, pp. 13–21.

[32] Newton MS cited in *The Correspondence of Isaac Newton*, ed. H. W. Turnbull *et al.*, 7 vols. (Cambridge, 1959–77), Vol. 5, p. 300.

[33] Newton, *Principia*, p. 298.

34 Newton to Bentley, 25 February 1692/3, *Correspondence*, Vol. 3, p. 254.
35 Whiteside, ed., *Mathematical Papers*, Vol. 6, pp. 93, 191.
36 Newton, *Opticks*, pp. 397–401.
37 J. E. McGuire, 'Force, active principles and Newton's invisible realm', *Ambix*, 15 (1968), 171. See also G. Buchdahl, 'Explanation and gravity', in *Changing Perspectives in the History of Science*, ed. M. Teich and R. M. Young (London, 1973), pp. 167–203.
38 Newton, *Opticks*, pp. 399–401; Newton MS in McGuire, 'Force, active principles', p. 196.
39 Newton, *Opticks*, p. 380; Newton MS in McGuire, 'Force, active principles', p. 171.
40 Newton MS in McGuire, 'Force, active principles', p. 171.
41 *Correspondence*, Vol. 1, pp. 364–6.
42 *Cf.* J. E. McGuire, 'Transmutation and immutability: Newton's doctrine of physical qualities', *Ambix*, 14 (1967), 69–95.
43 Newton, *Opticks*, p. 401.
44 Leibniz to Newton, 7 March 1692/3, *Correspondence*, Vol. 3, p. 258.
45 Quoted in A. Koyré, *Newtonian Studies* (London, 1965), p. 141. See *Correspondence*, Vol. 5, p. 301 for details of the publication of Leibniz's remarks. Leibniz was referring to Newton's denial of occult qualities in the 1706 Latin edition of the *Opticks*: see *Optice* (London, 1706), p. 344.
46 Newton MS in *Correspondence*, Vol. 5, p. 300.
47 Newton, *Principia*, p. 765.
48 MSS quoted in McGuire, 'Force, active principles', p. 176, and H. Guerlac, 'Newton's optical ether', *Notes and Records*, 22 (1967), 48.
49 Newton, *Opticks*, p. 352.
50 Newton, *Principia*, p. 764.
51 Newton, *Opticks*, p. 362.
52 Newton, *Opticks*, pp. 351–2. *Cf.* Westfall, *Newton's Physics*, p. 395.
53 *Cf.* P. M. Heimann, 'Ether and imponderables', in *Conceptions of Ether*, ed. G. N. Cantor and M. J. S. Hodge (Cambridge, 1981), pp. 64–7, 81, for discussion of different interpretations of the ether.

CHAPTER III

Leibniz: the conservation of 'living force'

The concept of *forces* or powers (which the Germans call *Kraft* and the French *la force*) and for whose explanation I have proposed a distinct science of *dynamics*, to bring the strongest light to bear upon understanding the true *concept of substance*.[1]

§1. Leibniz and the mechanical philosophy

The disjunction between the activity of nature and the essential passivity of material entities gave Newton's natural philosophy an inherent tension. While explaining gravity in terms of a centripetal attractive force, Newton denied that the force of attraction was an inherent property of matter, appealing to the concept of active principles as a means of explaining gravity; yet active principles seemed to have an equivocal status as natural agents. Inertia was conceived as a passive property of matter, yet also as a power by which bodies resisted a change in their state of rest or motion.

It was to resolve the conceptual difficulties surrounding the concept of force that Leibniz aimed to establish a science of 'dynamics', which he envisaged as a theory of motion which was not based on a dualism of forces acting to bring about change and matter passively resisting change, but was conceived in terms of the agency of 'forces'. While Newton disparaged philosophical arguments, though nevertheless appealing to metaphysical foundations, Leibniz sought to explicate the relation between ontological foundations and the laws of empirical physics. Leibniz considered 'force' to be 'inherent in all substances', and in seeking to establish a more valid 'metaphysics and concept of substance' he aimed to establish the intelligibility of his theory of forces as physical concepts by emphasising the close connection between his science of 'dynamics' and the nature of substances.[2]

In *Specimen Dynamicum* (1695) Leibniz emphasises the metaphysical principles which establish the physical basis of his science of dynamics. He appeals to the law of causality, conceived as the equivalence of causes and effects, in support of his demonstration of the conservation of forces in nature. His theory of the motion and collision of bodies is based on an appeal to the law of continuity, that no change of motion occurs instantaneously but only by infinitesimal degrees. While the science of dynamics, in providing physical explanations of natural phenomena, does not appeal to the ultimate principles which determine the nature of substances, the justification of the conceptual rationale of the science of dynamics requires reference to the theory of substances and to metaphysical foundations. Leibniz thus emphasises that his theory of nature is grounded on sound metaphysical principles, contrasting the conceptual coherence of his science of dynamics with the ambiguities, as he sees it, of Newton's physics.

By contrast with Newton's natural philosophy, based on the supposition of the hardness and passivity of matter, of inertia as an essential property of matter, and on the disjunction between concepts of force and inertia, Leibnizian dynamics affirms the inherent activity of matter, defines bodies in terms of elasticity rather than hardness, and establishes the intelligibility of phenomenal forces by appeal to the status of fundamental forces as the defining characteristics of material substances. Leibniz also criticises Descartes' mechanical philosophy. He rejects the assumption that substances could be defined by their spatial extension; and he rejects Descartes' claim that extension and motion provide the conceptual framework for physical explanation.

There are two levels to Leibniz's theory of reality: first, the fundamental level of substances characterised by 'primitive' forces; and second, the phenomenal level of 'derivative' forces, whose operation explains physical phenomena, and whose intelligibility is justified by reference to a metaphysical explication of their relation to the fundamental 'primitive' forces. Leibniz's natural philosophy differs from Newton's not only in rejecting the Newtonian dualism between force and matter and in the adoption of a radically different theory of substance, but in grounding the 'new' science of 'dynamics', which Leibniz claims he has established, on a distinct concept of 'force' which, he maintained, was necessary to explain both the descent of bodies under the action of gravity and the collision of bodies, problems which had dominated the study of mechanics in the seventeenth century.

In Newton's physics the concept of force is defined by the second law of motion, in terms of the change of motion induced by an 'impressed force'. As Newton states it in *Principia*, the second law of motion states a proportionality between an impulsive force and a change of momentum, measured by *mv*, the product of the mass and the velocity of a body. While Leibniz does not reject the validity of the concept of momentum, or of the law of the conservation of momentum in the collision of bodies (and was aware of the work of Wren, Wallis and Huygens in clarifying these concepts),[3] he bases his science of 'dynamics', which is concerned with the agency of 'derivative' or phenomenal 'forces', on a concept he terms the 'living force [*vis viva*]', which is measured by mv^2.

The conservation of 'living force' became for Leibniz a fundamental law expressing the inherent activity of nature and the order and self-sufficiency of natural processes. Leibniz's writings did not however present a clear and systematic account of the law of the conservation of living force, but Johann Bernoulli published detailed discussions of Leibniz's ideas, drawing upon his extensive correspondence with Leibniz in elaborating Leibniz's theory of motion, though reappraising Leibniz's metaphysical arguments and theory of substance. Bernoulli's work provided a systematic account of the law of the conservation of living force in mechanics, a principle which was ultimately generalised (notably by Helmholtz) into the law of the conservation of 'energy', being transformed into a principle determining all physical processes.

§2. The development of Leibniz's science of dynamics

While Leibniz's mature formulation of his dynamics in his *Specimen Dynamicum* (1695) was undoubtedly shaped by his response to Newton's *Principia*, he had been developing the principles of his theory of physics since the early 1670s. In his *Theory of Abstract Motion* (1671) he expressed his dissatisfaction with Descartes' mechanical philosophy in terms which indicate a fundamental feature of his conception of the nature of physical explanation. He maintains that mechanical explanations based on the Cartesian principles of matter and motion could not provide an adequate account of physical reality. Descartes' mechanical models, while providing illustrations of reality, lacked the precision and rigour of geometry which was a necessary component of physical explanation. Leibniz wished to combine mathematics and the mechanical models of the mechanical philosophy so as to provide mathematically-precise representations of physical reality. He declares that '*Geometry*, that is imaginary, but exact; *mechanics*, that is real, but inexact; and *physics*, that is real and exact'.[4]

As explanations of reality Descartes' mechanical models have the status of hypothetical illustrations, demonstrating the possibility of subsuming physical phenomena under mechanical principles; while the physical principles of the model and the structure of reality are both grounded on the mechanical laws of matter and motion, the model is only a formal analogue of reality.[5] Leibniz therefore looked to a true science of nature, 'physics', which would overcome the insufficiencies of the Cartesian mechanical philosophy by describing physical reality with the rigour and precision of 'geometry'.

The mathematical methods which Leibniz believed were appropriate to the science of 'physics' were to shape his construction of his 'dynamics': the mathematics of infinitesimals. He was, however, as much of a neophyte in mathematics as he was in physics; as he later admitted, in his 'proud ignorance' he had yet to achieve his major insights into the nature of infinitesimal mathematics. Nevertheless his discussion of indivisibles in his *Theory of Abstract Motion* foreshadows his later and more sophisticated application of infinitesimal mathematics to the theory of bodies in motion. Leibniz seeks to apply the theory of indivisibles to the study of the motion of bodies, by applying the mathematical treatment of the relation between the continuum and its infinite number of infinitesimal parts to the problem of motion. He distinguishes between the infinitely small elements of motion, which he terms *conatus*, and motion (continuous change) itself, arguing that '*conatus* is to motion as a point to space, or as one to infinity, for it is the beginning and end of motion'. He thus treats motion in terms of the relation between the indivisible 'rudiments' of motion, *conatus*, and the continuum of motion.[6] The analysis of the motion of bodies in terms of the relation between infinitesimal and finite quantities was to be fundamental to Leibniz's mature science of 'dynamics'.

Leibniz does not enunciate the physical basis of his theory of motion in this treatise, and the first clear indication of his physics of motion is formulated in his 'Brief demonstration of a notable error of Descartes' (1686). Leibniz rejects the Cartesian measure of the 'motive force' of a body by its 'quantity of motion', measured by the size of a body and its speed of motion. By analysing the fall of bodies of different weights through various heights he establishes that the quantity of motion is not conserved in the fall of bodies under the action of gravity. Nevertheless, he declares that 'it is reasonable that the sum of motive power in nature should be conserved, and not diminished.'[7] Hence he concludes that the motive force of bodies is not measured by the Cartesian quantity of motion, because the quantity of motion is not conserved in all mechanical processes. Leibniz does not state a mathematical measure for motive force in this paper, but his mathematical argument implies that it is measured by the product of the mass and the square of the velocity of a body, a quantity which he later termed the 'living force' of a body, and whose conservation was a basic principle of Leibniz's dynamics.

Leibniz was familiar with Huygens' treatment of the conservation of the quantity mv^2 in collisions in a paper published in 1669;[8] and in the 'Brief demonstration' Leibniz alludes to Huygens' treatise on the pendulum published in 1673, where Huygens demonstrated the conservation of the quantity mv^2 as a consequence of the equality between the distance through which the centre of gravity of a body (or a system of bodies) will fall under the action of gravity, and the height to which it can ascend as a result of the velocity acquired in the fall.[9] From Galileo's law of falling bodies the distance of descent of each body is proportional to the square of its velocity, and the conservation of the quantity mv^2 follows from Huygens' 'chief principle of mechanics',[10] the equality of actual descent and potential ascent of the centre of gravity of a system of moving bodies. While Huygens' discussion of the problem clearly shaped Leibniz's argument on the fall of bodies in the 'Brief demonstration', Huygens had considered the quantity mv^2 to be a quantity without profound significance for the science of mechanics. By contrast, from the first Leibniz emphasises the special and universal significance of the conservation of motive force, its status as a fundamental 'natural law'.[11]

In the 'Brief demonstration' Leibniz declares that the 'motive force' of a body 'is to be measured by the quantity of the effect which it can produce', and in a reply to criticisms of his paper he amplified this remark. He states what he terms a 'metaphysical' axiom which 'provides the means of reducing the force to geometrical [mathematical] calculation'. This is the law of causality: 'we ought to establish . . . [a] law of nature which I hold as being most universal and most inviolable . . . there is always a perfect equivalence between the full cause and the total effect . . . each entire effect is equivalent to the cause'.[12] The equivalence of causes and effects in the science of mechanics is therefore expressed by the conservation of 'motive forces'; and the conservation of force cannot be measured by the Cartesian quantity of motion. Leibniz thus provides a metaphysical justification of the principle of the conservation of force, appealing to the law of causality.

Leibniz amplifies this argument in an unpublished 'Essay on dynamics' of 1692, where he brought together and extended the themes of his earlier discussion of the theory of motion and the conservation of force. He returns to his discussion of the ascent and descent of bodies, arguing that as much force would be required to raise a body weighing one pound to a height of four feet as to raise a weight of four pounds to a height of one foot. He maintains that this follows from the principle that 'the same quantity of force is conserved' which is itself grounded on the axiom of the law of causality, that 'the whole effect is equal to the total cause'. The equivalence between causes and effects is expressed by the conservation of 'force', which is measured by the weights of the bodies and the distances of ascent. He now states explicitly that the force of a body in motion is to be measured by mv^2, a quantity which provides a measure of causes and effects in the discussion of the ascent of weights, an example taken over from Huygens; and the conservation of the quantity mv^2, enunciated by Huygens, thus expresses the conservation of force.

Leibniz goes on to apply his discussion of motion in his *Theory of Abstract Motion* to the explanation of the nature of force. Following his earlier argument that the continuum of motion should be analysed in terms of the infinitesimal elements of motion, he now makes a distinction between the nascent state of motion and motion itself. This corresponds to a distinction between a force which arises in the tendency or 'effort [*conatus*]' of a body to achieving a state of motion, which he terms 'dead force [*force morte, vis mortua*]', and the 'living force [*force vive, vis viva*]' which arises in the actual motion of a body. The relationship between 'dead force' and 'living force' is that between infinitesimal and finite quantities, 'as a point to a line', and the living force is measured by the quantity mv^2. Taking the example of the descent of a body under the action of gravity, Leibniz argues that at the commencement of fall the motion of the body would be 'infinitely small'; but when motion is established the 'force has become living [force]', and the 'distances traversed in falling are porportional to the squares of the velocities'. Hence from Galileo's law of falling bodies, the force of the body would be measured by the living force, mv^2.

The explanation of the physical status of living force is therefore based on the mathematical relation between nascent and actual motion, on the relation between the infinitely small elements of motion and the finite continuum of motion. The science of dynamics is therefore based on the primacy of the concept of force, and Leibniz declares that it is 'force' that 'truly exists' and is 'most real'.[13] The new physics would be grounded on the methods of 'geometry' and would be both 'real' and 'exact', because the concept of 'living force', measured by the quantity mv^2, is explicated in terms of Leibniz's mathematical theory of motion, based on the concept of infinitesimals. Just as the principle of the conservation of 'force' was based on a metaphysical axiom, the law of causality, this mathematical theory of motion in which 'living force' is held to arise from an infinite number of infinitesimal impulses of 'dead force' is also based on a metaphysical principle, the 'law of continuity'. In a paper published in 1687 in reply to criticisms by Malebranche Leibniz had maintained that an acceptable explanation of the collision of bodies must not suppose that on collision bodies would pass instantaneously from motion to rest or from motion in one direction to motion in another direction, for this 'large leap from one extreme to another' violated the law of continuity.[14]

Leibniz developed this argument further in a letter to Johann Bernoulli in 1698. He stresses the implications of the 'law of continuity', the law that 'no change occurs through a leap', for the science of dynamics and the nature of matter. Leibniz asserts that the supposition of hard atoms would be incompatible with the law of continuity, which holds that 'no change occurs instantaneously . . . without passing through all intermediate degrees'. Hard bodies, being inflexible, would rebound after colliding with an instantaneous transition from one state of motion to another. The law of continuity implies that 'motion does not change by a leap'; hence the elasticity of matter and the Leibnizian theory of living force as arising from successive infinitesimal impulses of dead force were in consonance with the law of continuity.[15] Leibniz thus maintains that the metaphysical axiom of the law of continuity has its counterpart in mathematics and nature; a body would not change from one state of motion to another, from a tendency to motion to actual motion, without passing through all the intermediate degrees of motion, a physical argument which is grounded on the mathematical relation between infinitesimals and finite quantities.

Leibniz thus stresses the metaphysical foundations of his dynamics, appealing to his statement of the law of causality and the law of continuity in support of his mathematical and physical arguments. Moreover, in his short paper on the 'Correction of metaphysics' (1694) he maintains that the status of his concept of force was justified by its basis in his theory of substance;[16] and it was this problem that he confronts directly in *Specimen Dynamicum* (1695), emphasising the ontological foundations of his science of 'dynamics'.

§3. Leibniz's dynamics and theory of substance

In *Specimen Dynamicum* Leibniz seeks to elaborate the conceptual framework of the theory of motion that he claims is a '*new science of dynamics*'. This paper was the only detailed statement of his theory that he published, and in it he had two main and connected aims. First, to provide an account of his theory of substance, to emphasise the difference between his own and Cartesian and Newtonian assumptions about material reality. Second, to enunciate his theory of motion in terms of the concept of living force, to explain the distinct conceptual framework of his theory of the physics of motion, and the differences between his science of dynamics and Cartesian mechanical philosophy and the framework of physical theory presented by Newton in *Principia*. These two broad aims were closely connected, for it was Leibniz's thesis that an understanding of the concept of force in physics requires analysis of the relationship between phenomenal forces and the fundamental or 'primitive' forces which characterise the nature of substances.

Thus while the concept of force has a secondary role in Descartes' mechanical philosophy, and a central—but to Leibniz ambiguous—status in Newton's physics, Leibniz seeks to clarify the status of force as the primary agent in nature, by emphasising that his dynamics was based on his theory of substance. Leibniz declares that it is 'the character of substances to act' and that the extension of bodies is merely the 'continuation or diffusion' of an acting or resisting substance. Hence a 'natural force' which gives rise to the inherent activity of substances is 'prior to extension' in bodies, and 'force' constitutes the 'inmost nature of bodies'. Spatial extension is therefore conceived as a manifestation of substance, not its defining property. Leibniz argues that motion is relational, being merely a process of continuous change in space and time; motion merely represents a continuous change of situation.

Hence motion could not be considered as 'real'; indeed motion, strictly speaking, does not exist being merely a 'momentaneous state', a state in which force acts.[17] He concludes that 'force' is the most basic concept defining the nature of substances: something besides 'magnitude and impenetrability' characterises bodies, and the realisation of this leads to an 'examination of forces'.[18] In a letter to de Volder in 1699 he explained that the basis of reality was an 'active principle, which was the 'substantial and constitutive' basis of bodies endowed with extension, and of which extension was an 'attribute'.[19]

In *Specimen Dynamicum* Leibniz distinguishes between 'active' and 'passive' forces and between 'primitive' and 'derivative' forces. He uses scholastic terminology in characterising 'primitive' forces, referring to the primitive active force as the 'soul or the substantial form' and to the primitive passive force as the 'prime matter', the Aristotelian primary matter, the substratum of matter without form. He does however emphasise that he is not returning to Aristotelian explanations of phenomena, for though the concept of substantial forms had the 'function of revealing the sources of things' such concepts could not explain the 'peculiar and special causes of sensible things'. Leibniz here expresses a fundamental feature of his metaphysics, that the 'crude concept of corporeal substance' supposed by the Cartesian mechanical philosophy could not explain the nature of substances. Nevertheless the primitive forces related 'only to general causes, which could not suffice to explain phenomena': it was derivative forces which were concerned with the 'reasons for the laws of nature'.

The science of dynamics is therefore concerned with derivative forces, the 'force by which bodies act on one another or are acted upon by each other'. While primitive forces characterise the nature of substances, derivative forces act to produce motion. Derivative forces arise through a 'limitation' of primitive forces; hence the conceptual status and intelligibility of derivative forces is grounded on their relation to primitive forces and to the nature of substances. The derivative active forces, living force and dead force, and the derivative passive forces, the impenetrability of bodies and their resistance to motion, are thus the phenomenal manifestations of primitive forces.[20]

A derivative force such as living force is thus considered to be phenomenal; while it is part of the order of nature and determines the laws of nature it does not possess the status of the primitive forces which characterise the nature of substances.[21] The derivative forces such as living force which alone provide the basis for physical theorising are thus phenomenal analogues of the primitive forces which define the essential nature of substances. The disjunction between substances and phenomena has as its counterpart the distinction between primitive forces which explain the ultimate 'sources of things' and derivative forces which explain the 'laws of nature', the 'phenomena' of physics. Hence Leibniz's distinct concepts of living and dead force, which are basic to his dynamics, are rendered conceptually intelligible by appeal to the analogy between substances and phenomena, between primitive and derivative forces.

The concept of living force is therefore only intelligible in terms of this metaphysical explication of the relation between primitive forces *qua* substances and derivative forces which explain the motions and collisions of bodies, yet the restriction of the science of dynamics to the formulation of the physics of derivative forces is basic to Leibniz's programme of scientific explanation. He declares that science is concerned with the 'immediate and special efficient causes of natural things', and hence reference to the 'first and most universal efficient cause [God]' is inappropriate in the treatment of scientific problems. Leibniz thus emphasises a sharp disjunction between the explanation of phenomena by 'mechanical efficient causes' and the 'general and remote' principles by which the order of nature is constructed; yet he maintains that these 'mechanical laws' are derived from 'higher reasons'. While Leibniz stresses the metaphysical foundations of his theory of dynamics and its basis in his theory of substance, he emphasises both the sufficiency (for purposes of the scientific explanation of phenomena by mechanical laws) and the phenomenal status of his physics of derivative forces.

Leibniz therefore rejects any claim that there are certain natural phenomena that 'cannot be explained mechanically'. He appeals to the metaphysical axiom that there is 'neither more nor less power contained in the effect than in the cause' in support of his contention that 'living force' will be conserved in bodies, emphasising that the laws of nature are explicable in terms of the operations of phenomenal derivative forces. He also maintains that his dynamics is based on the 'systematic' rule of motion that 'all change occurs gradually'.[22] This law of continuity is of especial importance in his discussion of the way in which living force arises from 'an infinite number of continuous impressions of dead force'. In discussing his explanation of living force as being produced by an infinite number of infinitesimal impulses of dead force Leibniz remarks that in referring to infinitesimal quantities he did not mean to imply that these 'mathematical entities' were 'really found in nature'; he merely employed them as a means of making calculations.[23]

This argument is in accordance with his general view of the existential status of infinitesimals. Writing to Bernoulli in 1698, he declared that 'infinitesimals are imaginary [quantities]' and did 'not exist in nature';[24] while he emphasised to Varignon in 1702 that infinitesimally small quantities were to be considered as 'ideal entities, or as well-founded fictions', even though 'everything takes place, in geometry, and even more in nature, as if they [infinitesimals] were perfect realities'.[25] While the mathematical model of the generation of living force from infinitesimal impulses of dead force provides an 'ideal' representation of nature, Leibniz stresses the status of living force itself as a real and conserved dynamical quantity, though not possessing the status of primitive forces which characterise the nature of substance. The subsumption of living forces under the law of causality, the equivalence of causes and effects, a metaphysical axiom which established the conservation of living forces in nature, established living force as a phenomenal analogue of the primitive forces which defined substances.[26]

Leibniz thus formulates a science of 'dynamics' which demonstrates both the sufficiency of physical concepts as providing explanations of phenomena, as well as tracing out the links between these 'functional' representations and their basis in the theory of substances.

§4. Leibniz and Clarke on conservation and attraction

The framework of natural philosophy which Leibniz proposed in *Specimen Dynamicum* shows striking contrasts to Newton's theory of nature in *Principia* and the *Opticks*. Leibniz emphasises the self-sufficiency of nature in terms of the conservation of living force, stressing the inherent activity of nature and the elasticity of matter; whereas Newton appeals to 'active principles' which serve to regenerate the activity of nature, and stresses the hardness and passivity of matter. Whereas Leibniz argues that the force of gravity can be explained by a mechanical model based on the circulation of material vortices, Newton appeals to the concept of centripetal attractive force, a concept which seemed to Leibniz to be an 'immaterial and inexplicable power', lying outside the framework of physical theory.[27]

These issues were fully discussed in Leibniz's correspondence with Newton's spokesman Samuel Clarke in 1715–16.[28] Leibniz criticises Newton's theory of 'active principles' which, he declares, seems to imply that God is obliged to 'clean' and 'even to mend' the 'machine' of nature, a doctrine which 'will not sufficiently show his *wisdom*'. Because the attraction of planetary bodies 'cannot be explained by the nature of bodies', that is by a mechanical explanation, this concept of attraction is 'a miraculous thing'. Attraction is therefore 'a chimerical thing, a scholastic occult quality'; and in supposing that God regenerates the activity of nature by means of active principles Newton has implied a 'supernatural' doctrine, in supposing that 'the whole universe of bodies should receive a new force'. By contrast Leibniz points to his own dynamical principle that 'the same force and vigour remains always in the world, and only passes from one part of matter to another, agreeably to the laws of nature, and the beautiful pre-established order'.[29] The principle of the conservation of living force is thus in consonance with the harmony and order of the cosmos and with divine omniscience in creating a universe operating according to the perfect and self-sufficient laws established at creation.

Newton and Clarke however reject Leibniz's criticism of the concept of attraction as a concept lying outside the framework of natural laws. Clarke argues that attraction is 'natural' because it acts 'regularly and constantly' according to the law of gravity; because phenomena cannot be subsumed under the principles of mechanism does not render them unintelligible or supernatural. Gravity acts regularly and according to demonstrated mathematical laws, and hence 'gravitation may be effected by regular and natural powers, though they be not mechanical'. Clarke also rejects Leibniz's doctrine of the conservation of living force on theological grounds. He maintains that to deny that 'every action is the giving of a new force to the thing acted upon', as Leibniz supposes, would be to imagine that God is 'quite excluded from the government of the natural world'. Leibniz's doctrine of the self-sufficiency of forces in nature has as its consequence the denial of God's presence and governance of the natural order. By contrast, Clarke declares, the Newtonian doctrine that 'there must be a continual increase and decrease of the whole quantity of motion in the universe' has the consequence that 'every thing be not mere absolute mechanism'.[30] The insufficiency of mechanical explanations thus is seen as demonstrating divine superintendence of the natural order. These physico-theological arguments provide a rationale for the Newtonian disparagement of Leibniz's physical theories.

The correspondence between Leibniz and Clarke gave public expression to the disagreement between Newton and Leibniz about active principles and the status of the concept of gravitational attraction. One likely motive for Newton's inclusion of the ether model in the 1717 *Opticks* was to refute Leibniz's criticism of Newton's concept of gravity as an 'occult quality', by providing a physical illustration of an active principle establishing the intelligibility of the distance force of gravity.

The correspondence also reawakened Johann Bernoulli's interest in Leibnizian dynamics. The publication of *Specimen Dynamicum* had excited Bernoulli's interest and led to his lengthy correspondence with Leibniz on dynamics, which flourished in the late 1690s.[31] Bernoulli was deeply involved in Leibniz's priority quarrel with Newton over the invention of the calculus, which was in full cry at the time of the correspondence with Clarke, and in 1716 Leibniz drew Bernoulli's attention to his philosophical debate with Clarke and Newton, whom he considered to be his real adversary. Leibniz criticises Newton's doctrine of the 'spontaneous diminution of active forces and final cessation in the world', pointing out to Bernoulli that by the principles of Leibnizian 'dynamics', the 'same quantity of forces is always preserved'. In reply Bernoulli expressed agreement, developing Leibniz's own justifications of the principle of the conservation of forces. Bernoulli argues that 'no force is destroyed, without giving rise to an equivalent effect'; the 'effect is nothing other than the transformed force', and hence 'it is necessary that the same quantity of force be preserved'.[32] The appeal to the Leibnizian law of causality became a fundamental metaphysical presupposition of Bernoulli's theory of motion.

§5. Bernoulli's theory of motion

In 1698 Leibniz had stressed to Bernoulli that the law of continuity, the law that 'no change occurs through a leap', had profound implications for his theory of dynamics. Leibniz maintained that the mathematical law of continuity had its counterpart in the physical world. In reply Bernoulli accepted this argument, affirming that the law of continuity implied that all changes of motion occurred 'through all intermediate degrees . . . through successive increasing or decreasing quantities'.[33] The conceptual kernel of Bernoulli's treatise on the 'Laws of the communication of motion' (1727) was his adherence to the fundamental presupposition of Leibnizian dynamics, the law of continuity, and hence to the principle that the metaphysical axiom of continuity had its counterpart in mathematics and nature.

Following Leibniz, Bernoulli defines dead force in terms of an 'endeavour' or tendency to movement, as the force which a body not in motion receives when 'pressed towards motion'. An example of dead force is the force exerted by gravity, for 'at each instant, gravity impresses on bodies on which it acts, an infinitesimal velocity', and the resulting 'endeavour of gravity' is 'dead force'. While dead force is an infinitesimal impulse and is created 'instantaneously', 'living force is produced successively in a body' and hence 'time is needed to produce living force in a body'. Bernoulli thus follows Leibniz in supposing

that motion is produced in 'infinitely small degrees' in accordance with the law of continuity; therefore 'living force' is a
'finite and determinate quantity' and is produced as a result of
an infinite number of infinitesimal impulses of 'dead force', and
is 'inherent in a body when it is in uniform motion'. Bernoulli
also emphasises that the concept of infinitesimals had its
counterpart in nature, observing that the relationship between
'dead force' and 'living force' is analogous to the difference
between 'a line and a surface, or between a surface and a
solid'.[34]

The Leibnizian law of continuity, which implied the harmony
between the order of nature and the mathematical relation
between infinitesimal and finite quantities, is therefore a basic
metaphysical principle shaping Bernoulli's formulation of his
theory of motion. He notes the 'perfect conformity which
prevails between the laws of nature and those of geometry; a
conformity which is observed so constantly and in all circum-
stances, that it appears that nature has consulted geometry in
establishing the laws of motion'.[35] The Leibnizian concepts of
dead force and living force, and the theory of the generation of
living force from an infinite number of infinitesimal impulses of
dead force are therefore sanctioned by the harmony between
'geometry' and 'nature'. The 'law of continuity' is therefore a
'general law which nature observes constantly in all operations'.
The law of continuity provides an explanatory framework for
the problem of motion, having the consequence that all change
occurs by infinitely small degrees. Only by explaining the
transition of a body from a state of rest to a state of movement
in terms of a transition 'through all the insensible motions
which lead from one to the other' would it be possible to
explain the reason for the 'production of one thing rather than
another'. The law of continuity thus renders the order of nature
intelligible, establishing the 'necessary connection between the
two states' of motion and rest. Bernoulli thus echoes Leibniz's
principle of sufficient reason, explaining how the law of continuity renders the order of nature intelligible.

Bernoulli applies this theory of motion to the treatment of the
collision of bodies. Leibniz had pointed out to Bernoulli that
the law of continuity implied the elasticity of matter, and
Bernoulli maintains that the assumption of the 'absolute

hardness' of the elementary corpuscles of matter, as was assumed by the partisans of the atomic theory (notably Newton) was 'absolutely impossible'. He argues that if two hard bodies were to collide they would either come to rest instantaneously or would rebound in different directions to their original motions; and it would be 'contrary to the law of continuity' to suppose that bodies could either pass suddenly from motion to rest or from motion in one direction to motion in another direction without passing through all the intermediate states of motion. Newton's doctrine that hardness was an essential and universal property of matter, an assumption which was justified by the third rule of philosophising and the appeal to the metaphysical principle of the analogy of nature, is therefore in contradiction with the fundamental Leibnizian metaphysical principle of the law of continuity. Bernoulli thus emphasises that the law of continuity is an 'immutable and perpetual' general law of nature, establishing not only the manner in which the motions and collisions of bodies occur but also the essential nature of material substances.[36]

Bernoulli maintains that matter is inherently elastic, and that the hardness of a body is not to be conceived as a fundamental property of matter but as a relational condition. Matter is therefore fundamentally elastic and the hardness of bodies is explained in terms of the stiffness and rigidity of inherently elastic matter.[37] Bernoulli develops this theory of the essential elasticity of matter by applying it to the treatment of the transference of motion in the collision of bodies. Representing bodies as elastic springs, he supposes that motion is transferred between bodies by infinitely small degrees; hence motion develops 'successively and by elements', and can be considered as consisting of 'an infinite number of infinitely small parts'.[38]

In *Specimen Dynamicum* Leibniz had observed that the force manifested when a compressed elastic spring began to expand was an example of dead force,[39] and Bernoulli elaborated his discussion of the compression and expansion of elastic springs so as to provide a physical and mathematical representation of the relation between dead force and living force. He supposes that an elastic spring presses against a movable body, a ball, and argues that the pressure or 'endeavour' of the spring to expand is the dead force. As the spring expands living force is produced in the ball which is set in motion by the expansion of the spring. While the dead force will be proportional to the infinitesimal velocity imparted to the ball as the spring begins to expand, the living force will be proportional to the finite or 'actual' velocity of the ball. Bernoulli provides a mathematical demonstration of the relation between dead force as an infinitesimal quantity and living force as a finite quantity, and establishes the measure of living force as the product of the mass of the ball and the square of its velocity.[40]

Bernoulli thus provides a systematic account of Leibniz's theory of motion, based on the law of continuity and the principle that the mathematical concept of infinitesimals had its counterpart in nature, and justified by the assumption of the fundamental elasticity of matter, a theory of matter which (unlike Newton's concept of matter as characterised by the essential property of hardness) is grounded on the Leibnizian metaphysical axiom of the law of continuity. Bernoulli adduces further support for the theory of living forces by an appeal to the Leibnizian law of causality. The concept of living force is the true measure of force in nature because living force is 'equivalent to that part of the cause that is consumed in producing it'. Because 'the whole efficient cause is equivalent to the full effect which is produced', the conservation of living force in natural processes is consequent on 'the equality between the effect and the efficient cause'.[41]

Bernoulli stresses the conceptual significance of the conservation of living force as a fundamental law of nature. He contrasts his own, and by implication Leibniz's, statement of the law of the conservation of living force with Huygens' formulation of the conservation of the quantity mv^2 in collisions.[42] Bernoulli remarks that Huygens had regarded the theorem of the conservation of mv^2 as a mathematical proposition, a mere formula, without realising its fundamental status as a natural law. While Bernoulli was aware of the utility of the principle of the conservation of living force considered merely as a mathematical theorem, as a formula which could be employed in the solution of certain problems (such as the problems of vibrating strings),[43] he stressed the fundamental dynamical status of the law of the conservation of living force: 'without recourse to nature and first principles, the most important theorems degenerate into simple speculations'. Leibniz rather than Huygens had provided the conceptual framework for the science of dynamics. In his *Mécanique analytique* (1788) Lagrange observed that for Huygens the concept of the conservation of 'living force' was regarded as 'a simple mechanical theorem', but Bernoulli, who had adopted Leibniz's distinction between 'dead' and 'living force', had considered the principle of the conservation of 'living force' to be a 'general law of nature'.[44]

Bernoulli emphasises the principle of the conservation of living force as a fundamental natural law expressing the order and harmony of nature: if the quantity of 'living force', the 'single source of the continuation of motion in the universe' were not conserved, then 'all nature would fall into disorder'.[45] Bernoulli explicitly contrasts his Leibnizian expression of the self-sufficiency of nature as grounded on the preservation of living forces in natural processes, with the Newtonian theory of the diminution of activity in nature.[46] Based on the metaphysical principles of causality and continuity, and the harmony between mathematics and nature, the conservation of living force demonstrated the intrinsic intelligibility of nature.

§6. Bernoulli and Leibnizian metaphysics

Bernoulli presents his treatise on the 'Laws of the communication of motion' as a systematic elaboration of Leibniz's science of dynamics. Based on Leibniz's metaphysical principles of causality and continuity, the elasticity of matter, and the conservation of living force, Bernoulli's work provides a detailed presentation of Leibnizian dynamics, bringing together in a systematic and coherent fashion themes which Liebniz himself had never fully elaborated.

There are nevertheless some fundamental differences between Bernoulli's exposition of dynamical theory and the framework of physics outlined by Leibniz in *Specimen Dynamicum*. For Leibniz the intelligibility of derivative forces such as 'living force' was grounded on their status as phenomenal analogues of primitive forces which characterise the nature of substances, though derivative forces express the operations of natural phenomena. Bernoulli's discussion is confined to the physics of

Leibnizian derivative forces. In correspondence with Leibniz, Bernoulli had however shown an interest in Leibniz's theory of substance. In his initial response to *Specimen Dynamicum* in 1695 he had asked Leibniz about the concept of primitive force and about the relation between primitive force and the phenomenal manifestations of substances. He found Leibniz's discussion of metaphysical issues unclear, later complaining that Leibniz stated definitions rather than giving explanations. In response to this complaint that his treatment of metaphysical issues was too laconic Leibniz made considerable efforts to explain his views to Bernoulli; but while Bernoulli concurred in the view that natural bodies arose from the interaction of 'primitive and innate' forces,[47] the intricate Leibnizian metaphysical justification of derivative forces as phenomenal analogues of the primitive forces which defined the nature of substances, yet being conceived as part of the order of nature and expressing the laws of nature, played no part in Bernoulli's exposition of dynamics.

Bernoulli's discussion of dead force and living force implies the rejection of the categories of Leibniz's ontology. Bernoulli and Leibniz had discussed the problem of the existential status of infinitesimals in a series of letters in 1698–9, and Bernoulli rejected Leibniz's view that infinitesimals were imaginary, declaring that 'the infinitesimal exists'.[48] In *Specimen Dynamicum* Leibniz had remarked that the infinitesimals posited in his dynamics did not possess the status of physical entities but were merely mathematical quantities, providing a mathematical representation of nature. Bernoulli's view of the ontological status of infinitesimals and his assumption of the harmony between mathematics and nature thus implies the physical reality of dead force in his dynamics.

This interpretation of dead force as a physical quantity is in consonance with Bernoulli's discussion of the ontological status of living force in his essay 'On the true concept of living forces' (1735). He asserts that living force is to be considered as a 'power of acting' for it subsists in matter even if it is not actually manifested. 'Living force' is 'a real and substantial entity, which subsists in itself inasmuch as it is in to do so [*quantum in se est*]'. Bernoulli is almost certainly echoing Descartes and Newton in using the phrase *quantum in se est*. Just as Newton had employed this expression to stress the status of inertia as an innate and essential property of matter, which defined the natural tendency of a body to remain in a state of rest or motion, Bernoulli uses this phrase to emphasise the conceptual status of living force as a power of acting which is inherent in moving bodies or elastic springs, a fundamental 'absolute' quantity which is 'always conserved'.

Bernoulli's theory of living force as a 'real and substantial entity' contrasts with Leibniz's concept of living force as a physical quantity which is a phenomenal analogue of the primitive forces which define substances. Bernoulli emphasises the status of living force as an existent quantity which is inherent in substances. By implication both dead force and living force have the status of real, existent quantities, though their dynamical status is quite distinct. While dead force is transient, living force remains in existence and is conserved and never diminished.[49]

In a letter to his former pupil Euler in 1737, commenting on the title of Euler's *Mechanica* (1736), Bernoulli remarked that he preferred the term 'dynamics' that Leibniz had employed to refer to the phenomena in which living force is manifested.[50] While Bernoulli's dynamical writings show his rejection of the categories of Leibniz's ontology, Bernoulli bases his theory of motion on the Leibnizian metaphysical axioms of continuity and causality, principles which established the intelligibility of his theory of motion and the conceptual rationale of his conservation law. Moreover, Bernoulli emphasises the self-sufficiency and conservation of nature, and follows Leibniz in rejecting the Newtonian theory of the dissipation of activity in nature.

The principle of the harmony between nature and mathematics and the law of the conservation of living force (which established the self-sufficiency of nature) provide the conceptual structure of Bernoulli's and Leibniz's physics. Grounded on an explicit appeal to metaphysical principles, the axioms of continuity and causality, the Leibnizian science of dynamics claimed to provide a systematic and intelligible natural philosophy. Leibniz aimed to provide coherent metaphysical foundations for physical concepts, and to explicate the relationship between physical explanations and the nature of substances, enunciating a natural philosophy which denied the confused premises and conceptual ambiguities of Newton's theory of nature.

Notes

1 G. W. Leibniz, 'De primae philosophiae emendatione, et de notione substantiae', *Die philosophischen Schriften*, ed. C. I. Gerhardt, 7 vols. (Berlin, 1875–90), Vol. 4, p. 469.
2 Leibniz, *Philos. Schriften*, Vol. 4, pp. 468–70.
3 G. W. Leibniz, *Mathematische Schriften*, ed. C. I. Gerhardt, 7 vols. (Berlin, 1849–63). Vol. 3, pp. 69, 260–1; *ibid.*, voi. 6, p. 227. For the statement of the conservation of momentum see especially the paper by C. Huygens, 'Régles du mouvement dans la recontre des corps', *Phil. Trans.*, 4 (1669), 925–8.
4 Leibniz, *Theoria motus abstracti* [1671], *Math. Schriften*, Vol. 6, p. 74.
5 G. Buchdahl, *Metaphysics and the Philosophy of Science* (Oxford, 1969), pp. 142–4.
6 Leibniz, *Math. Schriften*, Vol. 3, p. 72 n; *ibid.*, Vol. 6, p. 68. On indivisibles see J. E. Hofmann, *Leibniz in Paris 1672–1676* (Cambridge, 1974), p. 8. On *conatus* see M. Gueroult, *Leibniz: dynamique et métaphysique* (Paris, 1967), pp. 70–5.
7 G. W. Leibniz, 'Brevis demonstratio erroris memorabilis Cartesii' [1686], *Math. Schriften*, Vol. 6, p. 117.
8 Huygens, 'Régles du mouvement'.
9 C. Huygens, *Horologium oscillatorium* [1673], *Oeuvres complètes*, 22 vols. (The Hague, 1888–1950), Vol. 18, pp. 147, 247, 255.
10 Huygens, *Oeuvres*, Vol. 8, p. 499.
11 Leibniz, *Math. Schriften*, Vol. 6, p. 117.
12 Leibniz, reply to Catelan [1687], *Philos. Schriften*, Vol. 3, pp. 45–6. *Cf.* C. Iltis, 'Leibniz and the *vis viva* controversy', *Isis*, 62 (1971), 21–35.
13 Leibniz, unpublished 'Essay de dynamique' [1692], in P. Costabel, *Leibniz et la dynamique* (Paris, 1960), pp. 97–106.
14 Leibniz, reply to Malebranche [1687], *Philos. Schriften*, Vol. 3, p. 53.
15 Leibniz to Bernoulli, 20/30 September 1698, *Math. Schriften*, Vol. 3, p. 544.
16 Leibniz, *Philos. Schriften*, Vol. 4, p. 469.
17 G. W. Leibniz, 'Specimen dynamicum' [1695], *Math. Schriften*, Vol. 6, pp. 234–5. I have consulted the translation by L. E. Loemker in Leibniz, *Philosophical Papers and Letters* (Dordrecht, 1969), pp. 435–44.
18 Leibniz, *Math. Schriften*, Vol. 6, p. 241.
19 Leibniz to de Volder, 23 June 1699, *Philos. Schriften*, Vol. 2, p. 184.
20 Leibniz, *Math. Schriften*, Vol. 6, pp. 236–8.
21 Buchdahl, *Metaphysics and the Philosophy of Science*, p. 410.
22 Leibniz, *Math. Schriften*, Vol. 6, pp. 241–3.
23 Leibniz, *Math. Schriften*, Vol. 6, p. 238.
24 Leibniz to Bernoulli, 7 June and 18 November 1698, *Math. Schriften*, Vol. 3, pp. 499, 551.

[25] Leibniz to Varignon, 20 June and 2 February 1702, *Math. Schriften*, Vol. 4, pp. 110, 93. On infinitesimals see J. Mittelstrass, *Neuzeit und Aufklärung*, (Berlin, 1970), pp. 489–501.

[26] See also J. E. McGuire, '"Labryinthus continui": Leibniz on substance, activity, and matter', in *Motion and Time, Space and Matter*, ed. P. K. Machamer and R. G. Turnbull (Columbus, Ohio, 1976), pp. 290–326.

[27] Leibniz to Huygens, 13 October 1690, *Math. Schriften*, Vol. 6, p. 189. On Leibniz's celestial mechanics see E. J. Aiton, *The Vortex Theory of Planetary Motions* (London, 1972), pp. 125–51.

[28] A. Koyré and I. B. Cohen, 'Newton and the Leibniz-Clarke correspondence', *Arch. Int. d'Hist. Sci.*, 15 (1962), 63–126; F. E. L. Priestley, 'The Clarke-Leibniz controversy', in *The Methodological Heritage of Newton*, ed. R. E. Butts and J. W. Davis (Oxford, 1970), pp. 34–56.

[29] *The Leibniz-Clarke Correspondence*, ed. H. G. Alexander (Manchester, 1956), pp. 12, 18, 30, 86, 94.

[30] *Leibniz-Clarke Correspondence*, pp. 51, 53, 110.

[31] P. M. Heimann, '"Geometry and nature": Leibniz and Johann Bernoulli's theory of motion', *Centaurus*, 21 (1977), 1–26.

[32] Leibniz to Bernoulli, 7 June 1716, and Bernoulli to Leibniz, 14 July 1716, *Math. Schriften*, Vol. 3, pp. 964, 966.

[33] Leibniz to Bernoulli, 20/30 September 1698, and Bernoulli to Leibniz, 8 November 1698, *Math. Schriften*, Vol. 3, pp. 544, 548.

[34] J. Bernoulli, 'Discours sur les lois de la communication du mouvement' [1727], *Opera Omnia*, 4 vols. (Lausanne, 1742), Vol. 3, pp. 23, 35, 36, 38, 39. *Cf.* Leibniz to de Volder (undated, late 1698), *Philos. Schriften*, Vol. 2, p. 154, comparing 'living force' to 'dead force' as a 'line' to its 'elements'.

[35] Bernoulli, *Opera*, Vol. 3, p. 58.

[36] Bernoulli, *Opera*, Vol. 3, pp. 9–10.

[37] Bernoulli, *Opera*, Vol. 3, pp. 13, 14, 81. On Bernoulli's physical model of matter see C. Iltis, 'The decline of Cartesianism in mechanics', *Isis*, 64 (1973), 363–6.

[38] Bernoulli, *Opera*, Vol. 3, pp. 15–16.

[39] Leibniz, *Math. Schriften*, Vol. 6, p. 238. *Cf.* Leibniz to Bernoulli, 24 June 1695, *Math. Schriften*, Vol. 3, pp. 193–4.

[40] Bernoulli, *Opera*, Vol. 3, pp. 45–7. For the details of the argument see Heimann, 'Geometry and nature', pp. 14–15, 25.

[41] Bernoulli, *Opera*, Vol. 3, p. 38.

[42] C. Huygens, *De motu corporum ex percussione* [*Christiani Huygeni Opuscula Posthuma*, ed. B. de Volder and B. Fullenius (Leiden, 1703)], *Oeuvres*, Vol. 16, p. 73. Bernoulli was familiar with this work: see *Opera*, Vol. 3, p. 58 n.

[43] J. Bernoulli, 'Pro conservatione virium vivarum' and 'De chordis vibrantibus' [1727], *Opera*, Vol. 3, pp. 124–30 and 198–210.

[44] J. L. Lagrange, *Mécanique analytique* [1788], 2 vols. (Paris, 1965), Vol. 1, p. 226.

[45] Bernoulli, *Opera*, Vol. 3, p. 58.

[46] Bernoulli, *Opera*, Vol. 3, p. 40.

[47] Bernoulli to Leibniz, 8/18 June 1695, 8 November 1698, and 6 December

1698, *Math. Schriften*, Vol. 3, pp. 188, 545, 547, 556.

48 Bernoulli to Leibniz, 7 January 1699, *Math. Schriften*, Vol. 3, p. 563.

49 J. Bernoulli, 'De vera notione virium vivarum' [1735], *Opera*, Vol. 3, pp. 239–41.

50 Bernoulli to Euler, 6 November 1737, in G. Eneström, 'Der Briefwechsel zwischen Leonhard Euler und Johann I Bernoulli', *Bibliotheca Mathematica* (Series III), 5 (1904), 263–4.

CHAPTER IV

Kant: the metaphysical foundations of physics

All natural philosophers who wished to proceed mathematically in their work had therefore always (though unknown to
themselves) made use of metaphysical principles and were
obliged to make use of them, even though they otherwise
solemnly protested against any claim of metaphysics on their
science. . . . I believe that . . . perfection may in time be
attained by a cleverer hand when, stimulated by this sketch,
mathematical physicists may find it not unimportant to treat
the metaphysical part [of physics], which anyway cannot be
made superfluous, as a special fundamental part of general
physics, and to bring it into union with the mathematical
theory of motion.[1]

§1. Kant's metaphysics of nature

In the *Metaphysical Foundations of Natural Science* (1786), his
mature and most systematic discussion of natural philosophy,
Kant elaborates the ways in which the *a priori* categories of the
Critique of Pure Reason (1781), which he regarded as being
constitutive of all experience, were to be applied to the concept
of matter. In particular, Kant seeks to provide an analysis of
the conceptual framework of natural philosophy, the assumptions about 'matter' and 'force' which underlie Newton's statement of the laws of motion and the concept of universal
gravitation.

Kant's *Metaphysical Foundations* is of major importance in the
history of natural philosophy. Kant seeks to appraise the

relationship between Newtonian physical laws and the metaphysical assumptions which were fundamental to Newton's statement of these laws. Kant contests Newton's atomistic ontology and the doctrine that impenetrability and inertia were defining properties of matter. By defining matter in terms of inherent forces of attraction and repulsion Kant seeks to establish the fundamental status of the concept of force, which he believes is obscured in Newton's account, and to demonstrate the intelligibility of Newton's concept of the attractive force of gravity. Rejecting Newton's claim that inertia was an inherent power of matter, Kant seeks to clarify the status of the concept of inertia. By contrast with his early writings on natural philosophy, where he had emphasised the disjunction between mathematical and physical representations of nature, in the *Metaphysical Foundations* Kant aims to demonstrate the intelligibility of a unified natural philosophy by a metaphysical analysis of the conceptual foundations of Newtonian physics.

In emphasising that 'true natural science presupposes metaphysics of nature'[2] Kant argues that there are links between physical theory and the *a priori* principles of cognition. Kant's metaphysics of nature does not purport to claim that the actual inductive validity of Newtonian physics, the law of gravitation and the laws of motion, can be derived from *a priori* premises.[3] Kant's examination of the metaphysical foundations of Newtonian physical theory led him to a reappraisal of the conceptual status of 'force' and 'inertia', and to reject Newton's concept of inertia as a defining property of matter in favour of the ontological primacy of forces as characterising the essential properties of matter. Kant's account of the metaphysics of nature thus yields a framework of principles which differs from the metaphysical assumptions of Newton's natural philosophy. In seeking to establish the intelligibility of Newton's law of gravitation and laws of motion Kant provides a reappraisal of the conceptual structure of Newton's natural philosophy, reinterpreting the connection between Newton's physical theories and their metaphysical foundations.

In the Preface to the *Metaphysical Foundations* Kant makes a distinction between the general part of the metaphysics of nature (discussed in the *Critique of Pure Reason*), concerned with the general 'laws which make possible the concept of a nature in general', and the 'special metaphysics of nature' (the subject-matter of the *Metaphysical Foundations*), in which the *a priori* principles elaborated in the *Critique* are applied to the empirical concept of matter. He maintains that 'all true metaphysics is taken from the essential nature of the thinking faculty itself and therefore is by no means invented'. In the *Critique* Kant elaborated these *a priori* or 'transcendental' principles which provide the formal schema in terms of which the special 'metaphysics of corporeal nature' must be 'represented in accordance with the universal laws of thought'.[4]

By 'transcendental', as he explains in the *Critique*, Kant means the *a priori* 'categories' which establish 'the mode of our knowledge of objects in general'; these transcendental principles provide the cognitive framework which specifies the 'ground of the possibility' of all experience. The structure of nature is dependent on these categorial principles 'in respect of its conformity to law'. The category of 'causality', for example, as a transcendental principle, is regarded as a necessary ground for the possibility of 'nature' as such and of experience in general. 'Nature' is conceived as 'merely an aggregate of appearances' and as mind-related: 'we can discover it only in the radical faculty of all our knowledge'. 'Nature' is defined as 'the conformity to law of all appearances in space and time'. The categories therefore establish the lawlikeness of nature as a transcendental condition, by which experience is not only made possible but itself comes to possess a lawlike character. Kant argues that 'the order and regularity in the appearances, which we entitle *nature*, we ourselves introduce . . . [the] unity of nature has to be a necessary one . . . [so that the] subjective grounds of [this] unity [must be] contained *a priori* in the original cognitive powers of our mind'. The transcendental categories are therefore constitutive of experience, and Kant thus asserts that the principle of causality, the 'law of the connection of cause and effect', together with the other categories establish the lawlikeness of nature: 'nature . . . is dependent upon these categories as the original ground of its necessary conformity to law'.[5]

This conception of lawlikeness as a transcendental condition may be distinguished from the notion of lawlikeness according to which nature is held to be lawlike in the sense of being intelligible in terms of empirical scientific laws. Kant also argues that the possibility of the construction of a framework of theoretical science presupposes that nature be considered as being causally and systematically structured. Empirical laws are considered to be lawlike and hence necessary in the sense that their necessity relates to their scientific systematisation. Lawlikeness in this sense is a presupposition of the comprehensibility of empirical laws *qua* laws: 'without this presupposition we should have no order of nature in accordance with empirical laws'. Kant therefore distinguishes between the lawlikeness of nature as constitutive of experience and the lawlikeness of specific empirical scientific laws as a condition of the intelligibility of nature. Moreover, Kant emphasises that empirical scientific laws cannot be deduced from categories of the *Critique*: 'special laws . . . cannot . . . be *derived* from the categories, although they are one and all subject to them'.[6]

§2. Kant's *Metaphysical Foundations*

The purpose of the *Metaphysical Foundations* is to demonstrate the links between the transcendental categories and the laws of Newtonian physics, and hence to establish the intelligibility of Newton's law of gravity and the laws of motion. The metaphysical argument establishes the possibility of physical concepts and laws, not their physical actuality, and the discussion of metaphysical foundations is meant to yield principles of constraint on possible physical hypotheses, not to prove *a priori* the physical actuality of specific empirical laws. The metaphysical argument establishes physical laws and concepts as the empirical embodiment of the transcendental principles.[7]

In the *Metaphysical Foundations* Kant therefore elaborates a 'special metaphysics of nature' which considered matter as 'it must be represented in accordance with the universal laws of thought'. The four chapters of the book, 'Phoronomy', 'Dynamics', 'Mechanics' and 'Phenomenology' correspond to the categories of quantity, quality, relation and modality, which subsume 'all determinations of the universal concept of matter in general'.[8] While an early commentator maintained that the terms 'Phoronomy', 'Dynamics' and 'Mechanics' had little significance, deriving from Hermann's *Phoronomia* (1716), d'Alembert's *Traité de Dynamique* (1743) and Euler's *Mechanica* (1736),[9] Kant's terms do provide an indication of the structure of his argument. The term *phoronomia* had been used by Leibniz to denote motion as considered merely geometrically, precisely the sense of Kant's 'Phoronomy'.[10] The term 'dynamics' had clear Leibnizian echoes in the eighteenth century, and in the chapter on 'Dynamics' Kant is concerned to explicate the concept of force, though he does not seek to defend Leibniz's ontology of force. In the chapter on 'Mechanics' Kant is concerned to discuss the status of laws of motion, and the title of this chapter probably does relate to Euler's treatise on the science of mechanics.

In 'Phoronomy' Kant considers matter as being 'the movable in space', its only changes being those arising from its motion. Kant is concerned with matter viewed simply as an extensive magnitude, and with the construction of motion geometrically in terms of its velocity and direction. He derives rules for the composition of velocities with reference to the category of 'quantity', its subdivisions being unity, plurality and totality, arguing that the explication of motion in terms of the 'unity of line and direction' of different motions, the 'plurality of directions in one and the same line', and the 'totality' of motions in different directions and lines, establishes the intelligibility of matter viewed simply as an entity in motion.[11] As Kant emphasises, the metaphysical explication of the concept of matter proceeds in accordance with the transcendental principles of the *Critique*.

The analysis of the concept of matter in 'Dynamics' presupposes the concept of matter as being movable, but this is now supplemented by the property of resisting motion when its spatial extension is diminished. Matter fills space, according to Kant, by its repulsive forces, and the dispersion of matter is counteracted by an attractive force. The dynamical concept of matter is explicated in terms of the attractive force limiting the repulsive force, so that the repulsive force can vary in degree with regard to the same attractive force. The dynamical principle of repulsion is opposed by attraction and hence the perceptible degree of matter filling space is determined by the limiting or balance of the repulsive force by the attractive force. There is therefore a correspondence between these dynamical principles and the category of 'quality' (its subdivisions being reality, negation and limitation), which establishes 'the possibility of a space filled in a determinate degree'.[12]

In 'Mechanics' Kant is concerned to consider matter as 'the movable insofar as it is something having a moving force'. Kant attempts to analyse the relations of material objects with one another by means of their motions. The mechanical explication of matter presupposes the dynamical, for 'the communication of motion takes place only by means of such moving forces as also inhere in a material entity at rest'. The transfer of motion is explained in terms of the spatial changes of moving forces, and Kant is concerned to demonstrate the application of the category of 'relation' to the concept of matter. Kant's 'three laws of general mechanics', the 'law of the subsistence, the inertia and the reaction of matter', are concerned with the relations of material entities and 'exactly answer to the categories of substance, causality and community, insofar as these concepts are applied to matter'.[13]

In 'Phenomenology' Kant is concerned with the relation of matter to our experience of it. He states that matter can only be experienced in terms of its motion, that motion cannot take place without the influence of moving forces, and that the communication of motion depends on the relation between moving forces. Hence our experience of the motion of matter is determined with regard to phoronomy (motion), dynamics (moving forces) and mechanics (the relation of the moving forces), which provides an explication of matter 'with regard to its possibility, actuality and necessity, and hence with regard to all three categories of modality'.[14]

Kant's metaphysical 'construction of concepts' thus establishes the intelligibility of empirical physics based on the concept of matter. He maintains that the possibility of mathematical physics 'presupposes metaphysics of nature' because 'principles of the construction of concepts that belong to the possibility of matter in general must precede' and 'make possible the application of mathematics' to the concept of matter. Nevertheless he emphasises that the argument of the *Metaphysical Foundations* only purports to show 'the possibility of a mathematical theory of nature', not to demonstrate that matter can in actuality be represented by 'mathematical construction' along the lines suggested by Kant's metaphysics of nature.[15]

The argument of the *Metaphysical Foundations* is shaped both by the formal framework consequent on the application of the categorial principles to the empirical concept of matter, and by Kant's construal of the conceptual problems of natural philosophy. The conceptual status of force and inertia is at the core of Kant's treatment of metaphysical foundations, and in his 'metaphysico-dynamical' explication of matter in the *Metaphysical Foundations* he argues that forces are the defining properties of matter. While there are affinities between Kant's and Leibniz's critiques of Newton's theory of substance, in the *Metaphysical Foundations* Kant does not accept Leibniz's physics (based on the concept of living force) or his ontology; unlike Leibniz, Kant aims to establish Newtonian physical theory by a reappraisal of its metaphysical and ontological foundations. An understanding of the conceptual structure of Kant's metaphysics of nature requires an analysis of his discussion of the status of concepts of force and inertia, from his early writings on natural philosophy to the mature formulation in the *Metaphysical Foundations*.

§3. Kant's theory of living forces

In his *Thoughts on the True Estimation of Living Forces* (1747) Kant was concerned to analyse the arguments about whether the force of motion of a body was to be measured by the Cartesian 'quantity of motion' or by the Leibnizian measure of 'living force'. Kant was conversant with much of the extensive literature on this issue, notably the authoritative work of Johann Bernoulli, but he does not seem to have been familiar with the important critiques of the Leibnizian theory of living forces published by d'Alembert and Daniel Bernoulli in the 1740s. In any case, Kant's interpretation of the conceptual status of living force was quite distinctive, and differed markedly from the views expressed by d'Alembert and Daniel Bernoulli, that the theory of living forces should be regarded as a mathematical theorem rather than as a fundamental principle describing physical reality.[16]

Kant believed that the Cartesian measure of quantity of

motion could be established by mathematical argument, while the Leibnizian measure of living force, not being subject to the principle of the conservation of force (in Kant's view), was 'found to be false in mathematics'. While Kant disputed the mathematical status of the theory of living forces, he maintained that the Leibnizian measure of living force provided a true description of physical reality: 'I will maintain that living forces are really to be found in nature', he declared. Kant emphasised the disjunction between mathematics and physical reality, arguing that 'the mathematical concepts of the properties of bodies and their forces are quite distinct from the concepts found in nature'. There was therefore a gap between mathematics and nature, and Kant set himself the task of resolving this problem, maintaining that while living forces would remain concealed from mathematical argument they would be revealed by a 'metaphysical investigation', by which he meant an analysis of the ontological status of 'force' as a physical entity existing in nature.[17]

Kant quotes with approval Johann Bernoulli's view of living force, as stated in his essay 'On the true concept of living forces' (1735), as a 'real and substantial entity' persisting in natural bodies.[18] Kant observes that while Bernoulli had 'expressed his meaning as a mere geometer' his argument was nevertheless 'completely intelligible'; and Kant emphasises that 'this formulation expresses my view to no small advantage'. However Kant believed that Bernoulli was mistaken in seeking to establish the physical status of living force by appeal to the Leibnizian law of continuity, the mathematical relation between infinitesimals and finite quantities.[19] Kant criticises the Leibnizian distinction between the 'beginnings of motion' and 'actual motion', arguing that 'whatever is valid when a body has been in motion for some time . . . must also apply at the commencement of motion'. Assuming that there was a continuity and hence identity between the forces in these two states of motion, Kant rejects the conceptual basis of the Leibnizian distinction between 'dead force' and 'living force'. Kant turns the 'law of continuity' against Leibniz and Bernoulli, asserting that 'if a body possesses living force when it has been in motion for some time (for however small a time increment), then it must also have that force when it begins to move'.[20] He concludes that the Leibnizian mathematical measure of 'living force' was disproved by mathematical argument.

There are some parallels between Kant's critique of Leibnizian dynamics and arguments advanced by Euler in a paper on 'The force of impact and its true measure' (1745). Euler notes that according to Leibniz impact occurred in an instant giving rise to dead force; and that living force was held to arise from an infinite number of impressions of dead force. The two forces were therefore 'heterogeneous' (as Bernoulli, Euler's former teacher, had also expressed it).[21] Euler questions the heterogeneity of living and dead force by turning the doctrine of continuity against the Leibnizian argument. He states that according to this 'supremely constant law of nature, in virtue of which nothing occurs suddenly', impact would require a time interval; and so he argues that both living and dead force must arise in the same way, in a time interval, and hence have the same quantitative measure.

Euler concludes that 'the fundamental principle, on which rests the measure of living force, is not only unsteady, but falls entirely in ruin'.[22] Euler declares that Newton's first law of motion defined the measure of force, and in a similar fashion Kant concluded that 'mathematics does not permit a body to be endowed with a force . . . that is not the external cause of its motion . . . this is the fundamental law of mechanics . . . for which there is no other measure [of force] than the Cartesian'. In Kant's view Newton's first law of motion established the Cartesian measure of force by mathematical argument.[23]

Unlike Euler, however, Kant goes on to claim that a 'natural body' possessed a 'quite different property' from the property of inertia, the power by which a body perseveres in its state of rest or uniform rectilinear motion. This additional property of bodies, claims Kant, is the capacity of 'increasing in itself' the impressed force which was the external cause of its motion, so as to attain 'a degree of force that does not arise from the external cause of motion'. This property of physical bodies, Kant maintains, could not be reconciled with the mathematical theory of force: 'the mathematical concepts of the properties of bodies and their forces are quite distinct from the concepts found in nature'.[24]

Kant therefore stresses the disjunction between the mathematical status of force and its ontological status as an entity existing in nature; and he concurs with Bernoulli's characterisation of living force as a 'real and substantial entity'. In stressing the disjunction between mathematics and physical reality Kant poses the question: 'how is it that a law which is found to be false in mathematics can occur in nature?' To answer this question he provides a 'metaphysical investigation' so as to demonstrate the intelligibility of the concept of 'living force' as a physical quantity.

Kant explains 'living force' in terms of a concept which he terms 'intension', envisaged as the 'basis of activity' of physical bodies, representing their 'perpetual endeavour to action'. At the commencement of motion the striving towards motion is indeterminate, but once motion is established the 'intension' is finite. If 'force' is measured by the product of intension and velocity, which are each represented by a line, then once motion is established the force would be represented by a square, corresponding to the square of the velocity and the measure of living force as mv^2. While Kant attempts to 'connect the metaphysical laws with the rules of mathematics in order to determine the true measure of force in nature', seeking to bridge the disjunction between the mathematical and physical concepts of force, the gap between the mathematical and physical representations of nature was fundamental to the argument of Kant's treatise.[25]

In a later essay on *Physical Monadology* (1756) Kant sought to elaborate and develop his view of the ontological status of force. His argument probably reflects his response to the controversy over the Wolffian monad theory in the Berlin Academy in the late 1740s,[26] for he now asserted that bodies were constituted of 'monads' or 'simple substances' which possessed inherent forces which defined their physical reality. He supposed that the monads constituting physical bodies possess an inherent 'force of inertia'; and that while the 'inertia' of bodies was due to an inherent 'force', the contact action of bodies was explained in terms of the 'forces of impenetrability'. Kant here employs the Newtonian notion of attractive and repulsive forces to explain the properties of bodies. He argues that these forces are inherent in matter, and that the conjunction and degree of these forces determined the limit of the extension of bodies.[27]

In the *Metaphysical Foundations* Kant radically transformed the conceptual framework of his early natural philosophy, though he remained committed to one of the cardinal principles of the *Physical Monadology*, the primacy of force over the concepts of solidity and impenetrability. The central issue differentiating Kant's approach in the *Metaphysical Foundations* from his interpretation of natural philosophy in the essay on *Living Forces* is his commitment, in the *Metaphysical Foundations*, to establish the intelligibility of a unified natural philosophy, to bridge the gap between the mathematical and physical representations of nature.

In his essay on *Living Forces* Kant expounded his disjunction between mathematical representation and physical reality by contrasting the status of Newton's first law of motion and the concept of living force, the former expressing a mathematical law of nature while living force was conceived as an active inherent force persisting in natural bodies. In seeking to unify the mathematical and physical representations of nature in the *Metaphysical Foundations* Kant rejects the concept of living force in favour of the concept of inertia, which he conceives as a law of mechanics which implied the passivity of matter, rejecting the physical theory of force propounded in *Living Forces*, that bodies possessed inherent activity. It is likely that this reappraisal of the conceptual status of force and inertia reflects Kant's indebtedness to Euler's critique of the Wolffian monadology and of the conceptual status of force, impenetrability and inertia in Newton's natural philosophy. Kant's restructuring of the relation between the concepts of force and inertia, which was fundamental to the argument of the *Metaphysical Foundations*, suggests the influence of Euler's critique of the expression 'force of inertia' in Newton's natural philosophy, an argument which Kant apparently echoes, even though Kant does not accept Euler's view that inertia was a defining property of matter, but continued to define matter in terms of attractive and repulsive forces.[28]

§4. Euler's theory of inertia

Euler gave a detailed analysis of the concepts of force and inertia in his *Letters to a German Princess* (1768–72). Euler agrees with Newton rather than Descartes in declaring that while extension was a necessary property of bodies 'extension and mobility alone do not constitute the nature of bodies', for 'something may be extended without being a body'. The property of 'impenetrability' was a necessary property of all bodies, without which 'extension cannot be body'. Impenetrability was the 'great spring by which nature works all her effects' because collision was the source of 'all the changes which occur in the world', and the motions of bodies were changed in collisions 'no more than is necessary to prevent penetration'.[29] In addition to the property of impenetrability, bodies possessed the property of inertia which was 'as necessary to bodies as extension and impenetrability'. Inertia is therefore a defining characteristic of material bodies: 'it would be impossible for a body to exist without inertia'.

Euler defines inertia as 'a repugnance to everything that tends to change the state of bodies'; hence there was a strict disjunction between the property of inertia and the concept of force which was the 'external cause' which was 'capable of changing the state of bodies'. Hence inertia was 'the opposite of a force', and the term 'force of inertia' which was employed by Newton was an abuse of language. Unlike inertia which was 'essential' to matter, force was not '*inherent* in matter'. Euler therefore rejects the Wolffian monad theory which held that bodies make a continual effort to change their state by means of an inherent force. In Euler's view this theory contradicted Newton's first law of motion and the property of inertia which was an essential and defining property of matter.[30]

Euler's theory of matter is fundamental to his explanation of the origin of forces. He maintains that collision, contact action, is the basic mode of change in nature, and the impenetrability of bodies was the source of the 'true origin of the forces which continually change the state of bodies in the world', for the impenetrability of bodies 'always exerts the force necessary to change their state . . . [so as] to prevent penetration'. The 'force' arising from impenetrability was only manifested in resisting penetration: 'it is only to prevent penetration that impenetrability becomes active'. Impenetrability was an essential property of bodies and the force to which it gave rise was dispositional: 'though impenetrability provides these forces' it was not 'endowed with a determinate force; it is rather in a condition to manifest force' necessary in order to prevent the penetrability of bodies. The concept of force was therefore explicated in terms of the more fundamental property of impenetrability which gave rise to forces sufficient to prevent the mutual penetration of bodies, and Euler declares that the 'origin of forces is based on the impenetrability of bodies'.[31]

In the *Metaphysical Foundations* Kant is in agreement with Euler in rejecting the doctrine that bodies make a continual effort to change their state by means of an inherent force, on the grounds that this doctrine contradicted the law of inertia. Kant's strictures against the term 'force of inertia', which he considers to be a linguistic and conceptual confusion, possibly reflect Euler's argument.[32] Kant does not however accept the Newton-Euler doctrine that inertia and impenetrability were essential properties of matter. In the *Metaphysical Foundations* Kant continues to affirm that the concept of force is ontologically prior to extension and impenetrability and that forces were the defining properties of matter. The discussion of the concepts of force, impenetrability and inertia in the chapters on 'Dynamics' and 'Mechanics' in the *Metaphysical Foundations* is fundamental to Kant's construal of the metaphysics of nature, and reflects a transformation in his interpretation of the problems of natural philosophy. Kant's argument in these chapters demonstrates his attempt to establish links between the categorial principles and the laws of empirical physics, in the context of his reconstruction of the relationship between the concepts of force and inertia and his reappraisal of the philosophical assumptions of Newton's natural philosophy, and his attempt to avoid the disjunction between mathematical and physical representation that had dominated his essay on *Living Forces*.

§5. Kant's theory of 'force'

In the chapter on 'Dynamics' Kant is concerned with the empirical concept of matter regarded as a movable entity filling space. In rejecting the doctrine espoused by Newton and Euler, that solidity and impenetrability were the defining or essential properties of material substances, Kant maintains that forces define the essence of matter, that force is 'inherent in matter'. The dynamical explication of matter thus supposes that 'matter fills a space, not by its mere existence, but by a special moving force'. Matter fills space by 'repulsive' or 'extensive' forces which resist the penetration of other forces and which thus form the 'basis of its impenetrability'. The property of impenetrability 'rests on a physical basis', for the 'extensive force makes matter itself as an extended entity, that fills its space, first of all possible'.[33]

Kant goes on to argue that 'the possibility of matter requires a force of attraction as the second essential fundamental force of matter', a force which limits the dispersive effect of the repulsive force. Without the attractive force, a fundamental or 'original' force which defines the 'essence' of matter, matter would 'disperse itself to infinity'; and without the fundamental repulsive force 'all parts of matter would approach one another without hindrance and diminish the space that matter occupies'. Hence the possibility of matter requires the assumption of an attractive force counteracting the repulsive force and establishing the 'limits of extension' of matter. Kant declares that 'repulsive force belongs just as much to the essence of matter as attractive force, and one cannot be separated from the other in the concept of matter'.[34]

This dynamical explication of the concept of matter is formulated with reference to the categories of 'quality' ('reality, negation and limitation'), which correspond analogically to the account of matter in terms of fundamental forces of attraction and repulsion which determine the 'degree of the filling of space' by matter. There is therefore a correspondence between the 'original attractive force' conceived as a 'penetrative' force which is counteracted by the repulsive force, leading to the 'limitation' of the repulsive force by the attractive force, and the categorial principles. The application of these categorial principles establishes links between the transcendental principles and the empirical concept of matter, and thus demonstrates the 'possibility' of the 'dynamical concept of matter as a movable entity filling space (in a determinate degree)'.[35]

Kant therefore maintains that his metaphysics of nature has exposed the falsity of the metaphysical assumptions which formed a concealed but nevertheless essential part of Newton's theory of nature. Kant rejects the concept of 'absolute impenetrability', the doctrine that 'matter, insofar as it is matter, resists all penetration unconditionally and with absolute necessity'. In place of this Newtonian 'mathematico-mechanical' concept of matter Kant proposes his own 'metaphysico-dynamical' mode of explanation, which supposes that impenetrability and extension are derivative properties of matter, being dependent on the fundamental forces which define the 'physical basis' of matter.

Kant argues that the repulsive force, which makes matter itself as an extended entity filling space possible, has 'a degree which can be overcome', and hence the spatial extension of matter can be diminished by a compressive force counteracting the repulsive force. Hence the filling of space by matter must be dependent on the 'degree of compression' or 'relative impenetrability' of matter. Thus the extension and impenetrability of matter could change by degrees of intensity, a theory of matter which is based on the dynamical explication of matter in terms of the fundamental forces of attraction and repulsion. This 'metaphysico-dynamical' concept of matter is shown to be possible by the application of the categories of quality to the empirical concept of matter. In contrast with Newton's 'mathematico-mechanical' theory of matter, according to which impenetrability and extension were absolute qualities defining the essential properties of matter and which could not change by degrees, Kant maintains that matter is to be explicated in terms of fundamental forces, demonstrating the 'possibility' of matter within the framework of his 'special metaphysics of nature'.[36]

Kant rejects the view of 'Lambert and others', presumably including Newton and Euler, who considered solidity to be a defining property of matter, an ultimate concept which entailed the absolute resistance of matter to penetration by other matter. He argues that the proponents of this 'mathematico-mechanical' theory suggested that solidity was a concept which could not be 'further constructed' because it was 'an initial datum of the construction of the concept of matter', and that they implied that solidity was 'incapable of any mathematical construction, so as to prevent a return to the first principles of natural science'.[37] Kant maintains that his 'metaphysico-dynamical' explication of the concept of matter has exposed the confused basis of this argument, by demonstrating that solidity and impenetrability were not ultimate concepts but were derivative, being grounded on the 'fundamental forces'. While he admits that the 'mathematico-mechanical' mode of explication had the advantage of explaining a great diversity of natural phenomena, he regards the conceptual foundations of this schema as being unsatisfactory.

Kant argues that his elaboration of a 'special metaphysics of nature' by the application of the transcendental principles to the concept of matter had established that 'force' was the 'initial datum' of construction. The 'metaphysico-dynamical' mode of representation of matter therefore contrasted favourably with the 'mathematico-mechanical' theory, for the latter was a 'merely mathematical physics' based on the 'empty concept' of 'absolute impenetrability', a conception of nature in which 'forces were philosophised away'. In the 'mathematico-mechanical' theory forces were arbitrarily superadded to matter, whereas the 'metaphysico-dynamical' mode of representation was based on the 'proper forces of matter' which were conceived as being essential to matter and as defining its materiality.[38]

Kant goes on to emphasise a key feature of his 'metaphysico-dynamical' explication of the concept of matter. He does not claim that this schema was intended to yield any specific empirical laws of forces, but declares that 'no law whatever of attractive or of repulsive force may be risked on *a priori* conjectures'. Kant's metaphysics of nature merely established the 'elements of the construction' of matter and provided no guarantee that matter could in fact be constructed in this way. He does not claim that the physical actuality of the forces follows deductively from the general categorial scheme. The metaphysical argument establishes only the possibility of matter in general as composed of 'fundamental forces' of attraction and repulsion, not that one can 'assume either of them as actual'. Kant emphasises that 'one must guard against going beyond what makes the universal concept of matter in general possible and against wanting to explain *a priori* the particular or even specific determination and variety of matter'.[39]

The 'mathematico-mechanical' mode of representation had the advantage in providing an explanation of a diversity of phenomena, as long as forces were supposed as acting. While the 'metaphysico-dynamical' schema was based on the concept of 'fundamental forces', which established a coherent metaphysical foundation for the concept of matter, Kant denies that his dynamical explication established the 'possibility of fundamental forces'. He declares that 'all means are wanting' for the construction *a priori* of the fundamental forces. Kant argues that forces cannot be constructed because they are 'fundamental' and 'cannot be further derived from any source', and also because they are empirical and are known from the 'data of experience' and cannot be exhibited *a priori*.[40] Forces can therefore only be 'assumed', and Kant does not claim to have established a mathematical physics based on the supposition of 'fundamental forces', but only to have established links between the categorial principles and the dynamical explication of matter in terms of the assumption of fundamental forces. In seeking to establish the intelligibility of a unified natural philosophy based on the 'fundamental concept' of force, bridging the gap between physical reality and the mathematical representation of nature, Kant denies that forces could be constructed, and thus emphasises that the metaphysical argument only establishes the 'possibility of a mathematical doctrine of nature'.[41]

Kant's 'metaphysico-dynamical' concept of matter provides the basis for a major conclusion of his metaphysics of nature, the justification of Newton's concept of gravitational attraction. Kant declares that the concept of 'universal attraction as the cause of gravity' together with the law of gravitational attraction must be concluded from the 'data of experience'. His intention is not therefore to derive the law of gravity from metaphysical principles, but to establish the intelligibility of the concept of gravitational attraction, to demonstrate its possibility. As Kant remarks, the justification of the possibility of the action of matter at a distance and of the 'concept of an original attraction' inherent in matter had given offence to Newton's contemporaries, and even to Newton himself. In emphasising that the 'possibility of matter requires a force of attraction' Kant sought to justify the notion of action at a distance as being 'possible without the mediation of matter lying in between', thus demonstrating the intelligibility of Newton's theory of gravitational attractive force.

The justification of the possibility of the concept of gravity is therefore given in terms of the 'metaphysico-dynamical' concept of matter, which supposes that 'matter occupies a space without filling it' by means of an attractive force. Hence the 'original and essential attraction of all matter is an immediate action of one matter upon another through empty space'. The attractive force is extended throughout the universe, and matter acts through space upon other matter by means of the fundamental force of attraction upon which the possibility of matter itself is based. By a conceptual explication of the concept of gravity, a major achievement of his metaphysics of nature and his reappraisal of the connection between Newton's physical theories and their metaphysical foundations.[42]

§6. Kant and the concept of 'inertia'

Kant's discussion of Newton's first law of motion in his chapter on 'Mechanics' is another important example of his treatment of the relationship between physical laws and metaphysical foundations. In 'Mechanics' Kant gives an account of the relationship between the concepts of force and inertia, seeking to clarify the conceptual framework of Newton's mechanics. The principle of causality states (as Kant expresses it in the *Metaphysical Foundations*) that 'every change has a cause'. Applied to the concept of matter it yields Kant's 'second law of mechanics: every change of matter has an external cause'. Kant places brackets round his appended statement of Newton's first law of motion to which this metaphysical 'law of mechanics' analogically corresponds, implying that the metaphysical argument merely establishes the possibility of Newton's first law of motion, not its physical actuality. His 'proof' of this 'second law of mechanics' does not purport to validate Newton's first law of motion, but to establish that all changes of matter are 'based on an external cause' and that matter 'undergoes no changes except by motion', suggesting a link between the category of causality and Newton's first law of motion. Newton's first law of motion is therefore construed as the empirical embodiment of the principle of causality, and the metaphysical argument establishes the possibility of a mathematical theory of nature.[43]

Kant describes his 'second law of mechanics' as the 'law of inertia', declaring that the 'inertia of matter is and signifies nothing but its lifelessness', its inability to 'determine itself to motion or rest as change of its state'. He argues that the doctrine that matter possesses an 'internal principle' or 'special force of matter under the name of the force of inertia' would contradict the 'law of inertia' which denotes the inherent passivity of matter. Kant's rejection of the supposition of an 'internal principle of a substance to change its state' was basic to his proof of the 'law of inertia'. He states that because 'matter has no absolutely internal determinations' hence 'all change of matter is based on an external cause'.[44]

Kant therefore agrees with Euler in rejecting the construal of 'inertia' as a 'special force of matter'. He maintains that the 'designation force of inertia' was self-contradictory; 'a special and entirely peculiar force merely to resist, but without being able to move a body, would under the name force of inertia be a word without meaning'. To suppose that matter possesses an 'internal principle' of 'inertia', which he considers to be implied by the term 'force of inertia', would contradict the 'law of inertia' which establishes that matter does not possess an inherent power enabling it to change its state.[45] Kant therefore rejects Newton's view of inertia as an inherent power of resistance conceived as an essential property of matter. For Kant inertia is regarded as a law of mechanics which implied the passivity of matter, not as a defining property of matter.

Kant's discussion of the concepts of force, matter and inertia is central to his account of the metaphysical foundations of Newton's theory of physics. While the application of the transcendental categories of the *Critique* to the concept of matter is shown to provide justificatory sanction for physical laws such as Newton's concept of gravitational attraction and first law of motion, Kant reconstructs the relationship between these physical laws and the assumptions about matter and force which underlie Newton's articulation of his physical theories. By seeking to enunciate more adequate metaphysical foundations for physical laws which are established by the data of experience, Kant intends to demonstrate the intelligibility of Newton's physics. The enunciation of Kant's 'metaphysico-dynamical' explication of matter thus serves to establish the possibility of Newton's concept of a gravitational attractive force; and the analysis of the metaphysical foundations of the concept of inertia clarifies the status of Newton's first law of motion.

§7. The construction of forces

In the *Metaphysical Foundations* Kant emphasises that he did not seek to establish the possibility of the fundamental forces of attraction and repulsion whose assumption provided the basis for his explication of the 'metaphysico-dynamical' concept of matter. The application of the categories of quality to the empirical concept of matter merely establishes the possibility of matter as explicated in terms of fundamental forces, not the physical actuality of the forces of attraction and repulsion. The gap between metaphysics of nature and the theories and laws of empirical physics is a key feature of the argument of the *Metaphysical Foundations*. In his later unpublished writings, known as the *Opus postumum*, written between 1786 and 1803 (though the bulk of the material was written in the late 1790s), Kant attempts to demonstrate the 'transition from the meta-physical foundations of science to physics', physics being defined as the study of 'matter and its moving forces under empirical laws of motion'. Kant thus aimed to demonstrate the link between the metaphysics of nature and the empirical laws of forces.[46] The first and most important part of this attempt to 'bridge' the 'gap' between the metaphysics of nature and empirical physics is to seek to demonstrate the possibility of 'the system of the moving forces of matter'.[47]

In the *Metaphysical Foundations* Kant had argued that the

fundamental forces could not be constructed because they were fundamental, and in seeking to demonstrate the possibility of the fundamental forces of attraction and repulsion he attempts to enunciate the ultimate ground of these forces. Kant remains committed to the 'physico-dynamical' theory of nature, rejecting the Newtonian 'corpuscular philosophy which explicated everything in terms of atoms and void space' as a 'nest of fabrications'.[48] Kant bases his construction of the 'moving forces of matter' on a metaphysical 'postulate', that the 'system of the moving forces of matter depends upon the existence of a substance' which is 'the universal basis of the moving forces of matter'.[49] This substance, which Kant terms the 'ether', does not have the status of a physical 'hypothesis' but is envisaged as a metaphysical 'principle of the possibility of the whole of experience'. Hence the construction of forces is grounded upon the concept of the ether as the 'principle of the transition', an 'infinitely continuous and internally moving matter upon which the possibility of all bodies depends'.[50]

Kant's introduction of the concept of the ether as the metaphysical principle of the construction of forces, and which would therefore demonstrate the possibility of the forces of attraction and repulsion, was probably influenced by contemporary criticism of the *Metaphysical Foundations*, which had questioned Kant's assumption of the repulsive force as a fundamental force of matter. Kant's concept of an inherent repulsive force as a defining and essential property of matter was criticised on the grounds that the repulsive powers of matter should be explained in terms of the elastic ether or 'caloric', the elastic substance of heat, this latter concept receiving full expression in the work of Lavoisier in the 1780s. Kant's assumption of a fundamental force of repulsion was criticised as being in conflict with current physical theory.[51] Kant referred to some of these criticisms,[52] and it seems possible that his reconstruction of his metaphysics of nature was influenced by the suggestion that a substance (ether or caloric, both terms being employed by Kant himself) could explain the repulsive powers of matter.

The supposition of a substance which could explain repulsion implied that the repulsive force was not 'fundamental', and hence that the possibility of forces could be established by construction. While Kant does not introduce the concept of a primordial substance as a physical theory of ether or caloric, it functions as the ultimate basis, the 'real principle' of the moving forces of matter. Kant conceives this primordial substance as having the property of perpetual motion, as being endowed with a 'primordial vibration'. He argues that the 'moving forces of matter must begin with some sort of motion', and hence the 'elementary substance' of the ether, endowed with inherent activity and motion, established the possibility of the fundamental forces of attraction and repulsion. He concludes that 'the concept of an elementary substance was [therefore] the basis of all possible perceptions of the moving forces of matter'.[53]

Having demonstrated the possibility of the forces of attraction and repulsion Kant has established the basis of the transition from the metaphysical foundations of science to physics, the science of physics being grounded on the moving forces of matter. He attempts to elaborate the connections between the empirical phenomena of physics and the moving forces of matter, employing the categorial framework of quantity, quality, relation and modality as a guide to the 'classification of moving forces inherent in all matter'.[54] Under quantity Kant discusses the weight of bodies in terms of opposing forces of attraction and repulsion; under quality he gives an account of the states and forms of matter (solidity, fluidity, crystallisation) in terms of forces of attraction and repulsion; under relation he discusses the mechanical properties of bodies, friction and cohesion; and under modality he emphasises the unity of the moving forces of matter as grounded on the concept of the primordial ether.[55] Empirical physics is therefore shown to be intelligible in terms of the laws of the moving forces of matter. Hence the 'totality of empirical laws of nature' is linked to the metaphysics of nature and shown to be intelligible in terms of the 'system of the moving forces of matter', which is itself grounded on the metaphysical principle of the primordial ether.[56]

In the *Opus postumum* Kant therefore tightens the links between the metaphysics of nature and empirical physics. But he does not thereby claim that the theories and laws of empirical physics can be derived from *a priori* premises. In discussing physical phenomena in terms of the classificatory schema of the categories Kant does not claim that the transcendental principles establish the physical actuality of specific empirical laws. The intention is rather to show that, having established the possibility of forces of attraction and repulsion by appeal to the postulate of a primordial substance, the phenomena of physics can be construed in terms of the categorial schema. The gap between empirical physics and metaphysics of nature is not closed by Kant's metaphysical construction of the moving forces of matter, but is merely bridged. The notion of a 'transition' between metaphysics of nature and empirical physics emphasises the significance of the disjunction between physics and metaphysics, and in seeking to elucidate the nature of this transition Kant reaffirms rather than denies the basic thrust of his metaphysics of nature as formulated in the *Metaphysical Foundations*.

In emphasising that the explication of the 'metaphysico-dynamical' concept of matter is central to the elaboration of metaphysical foundations, Kant sought to establish the intelligibility of Newtonian physics. By reappraising Newton's theory of matter, force and inertia, Kant made explicit the status of metaphysical foundations in Newton's theory of physics. Kant's argument highlights the centrality of the problem of substance in the explication of the metaphysical principles underlying Newton's theory of physics.

Notes

1   Immanuel Kant, *Metaphysische Anfangsgründe der Naturwissenschaft* [1786] in *Kants gesammelte Schriften*, Vol. 4 (Berlin, 1903), pp. 472, 478. I have consulted, though I have modified, the recent translation by J. W. Ellington of Kant's *Metaphysical Foundations of Natural Science* (Indianapolis/New York, 1970).
2   Kant, *Schriften*, Vol. 4, p. 469.
3   G. Buchdahl, *Metaphysics and the Philosophy of Science* (Oxford, 1969), p. 678.
4   Kant, *Schriften*, Vol. 4, pp. 469–73.
5   *Kant's Critique of Pure Reason*, trans. N. Kemp Smith (London, 1933), A25, B247, A114, A125, B165, B232.
6   1. Kant, *Critique of Judgement*, trans. J. C. Meredith (Oxford, 1928), p. 25; Kant, *Critique of Pure Reason*, B165. See G. Buchdahl, 'The conception of lawlikeness in Kant's philosophy of science', *Synthese*, 23 (1971), 24–46.
7   *Cf.* H. J. Paton, *Kant's Metaphysic of Experience*, 2 vols. (London, 1936), Vol. 2, p. 209; W. Stegmüller, 'Towards a rational reconstruction of

Kant's metaphysics of experience', *Ratio*, 9 (1967), 1–32; *ibid.*, 10 (1968) 1–37.

[8] Kant, *Schriften*, Vol. 4, pp. 473, 476, 477.

[9] *Gehlers physikalisches Wörterbuch neu bearbeitet*, 10 vols. (Leipzig, 1825–44), Vol. 2, p. 715. For a general discussion of Kant's terminology see H. Heimsoeth, *Studien zur Philosophie Immanuel Kants I*, 2nd ed. (Bonn, 1971), pp. 38–92.

[10] Leibniz [*Theoria motus abstracti* (1671)], *Mathematische Schriften*, Vol. 6, p. 71. *Cf.* R. Palter, 'Kant's formulation of the laws of motion', *Synthese*, 24 (1972), 111.

[11] Kant, *Schriften*, Vol. 4, pp. 480, 495.

[12] Kant, *Schriften*, Vol. 4. pp. 517, 523.

[13] Kant, *Schriften*, Vol. 4, pp. 536, 551.

[14] Kant, *Schriften*, Vol. 4, p. 558. On the framework of the *Metaphysical Foundations* see J. Vuillemin, *Physique et métaphysique Kantiennes* (Paris, 1955); H. Hoppe, *Kants Theorie der Physik* (Frankfurt, 1969); J. Ellington, 'The unity of Kant's thought in his philosophy of corporeal nature', in *Metaphysical Foundations*, pp. 135–218; G. G. Brittan, *Kant's Theory of Science* (Princeton, 1978).

[15] Kant, *Schriften*, Vol. 4, pp. 469–73.

[16] For relevant background see: T. L. Hankins, 'Eighteenth-century attempts to resolve the *vis viva* controversy', *Isis*, 56 (1965), 281–97; L. L. Laudan, 'The *vis viva* controversy: a *post-mortem*', *Isis*, 59 (1968), 131–43; R. Calinger, 'The Newtonian-Wolffian confrontation in the St. Petersburg Academy of Sciences', *J. World Hist.*, 11 (1968), 417–35; P. M. Heimann, '"Geometry and nature": Leibniz and Johann Bernoulli's theory of motion', *Centaurus*, 21 (1977), 1–26.

[17] I. Kant, *Gedanken von der wahren Schätzung der lebendigen Kräfte* [1747], *Schriften*, Vol. 1 (Berlin, 1902), pp. 139, 107, 60.

[18] J. Bernoulli, *Opera Omnia*, 4 vols. (Lausanne, 1742), Vol. 3, p. 240.

[19] Kant, *Schriften*, Vol. 1, pp. 150–1. *Cf.* E. Adickes, *Kant als Naturforscher*, 2 vols. (Berlin, 1924–5), Vol. 2, p. 98; Buchdahl, *Metaphysics and the Philosophy of Science*, pp. 553–6.

[20] Kant, *Schriften*, Vol. 1, pp. 37, 139.

[21] Bernoulli, *Opera*, Vol. 3, p. 37.

[22] L. Euler, 'De la force de percussion et de sa véritable mésure', *Mém. Acad. Sci. Berlin* 1 (1745 [published 1746]), 29–31. *Cf.* Colin Maclaurin, *An Account of Sir Isaac Newton's Philosophical Discoveries* (London, 1748), p. 132.

[23] Kant, *Schriften*, Vol. 1, p. 140.

[24] Kant, *Schriften*, Vol. 1, pp. 107, 140.

[25] Kant, *Schriften*, Vol. 1, pp. 139, 26, 141–8, 107. On the relationship between 'dead' and 'living force' as between a 'line and a surface' cf. Euler, 'Force de percussion', p. 29, and Bernoulli, *Opera*, Vol. 3, p. 37.

[26] I. Polonoff, *Force, Cosmos, Monads and Other Themes of Kant's Early Thought* (Bonn, 1973), pp. 77–89; R. Calinger, 'The Newtonian-Wolffian controversy', *J.H.I.*, 30 (1969), 319–30; J. Ecole, 'Cosmologie wolffienne et dynamique leibnizienne', *Etudes philosophiques*, 19 (1964), 3–10.

27 Kant, *Monadologia physica* [1756], *Schriften*, Vol. 1, pp. 473–87.

28 On Kant's relation to Euler see H. E. Timerding, 'Kant und Euler', *Kant-Studien*, 23 (1919), 18–64; for the context see Polonoff, *Force, Cosmos, Monads.*

29 L. Euler, *Lettres à une princesse d'Allemagne* [1768–72], *Opera Omnia*, Series III, Vol. 11 (Zürich, 1960), pp. 150–3.

30 Euler, *Lettres*, pp. 161–6.

31 Euler, *Lettres*, pp. 167–71.

32 Timerding, 'Kant und Euler', p. 50.

33 Kant, *Schriften*, Vol. 4, pp. 497, 502, 508.

34 Kant, *Schriften*, Vol. 4, pp. 508–11.

35 Kant, *Schriften*, Vol. 4, pp. 517, 518, 523.

36 Kant, *Schriften*, Vol. 4, pp. 501, 502, 525.

37 Kant, *Schriften*, Vol. 4, pp. 497–8.

38 Kant, *Schriften*, Vol. 4, pp. 498, 524–5.

39 Kant, *Schriften*, Vol. 4, pp. 517, 524–5, 534.

40 Kant, *Schriften*, Vol. 4, pp. 513, 525, 534.

41 Kant, *Schriften*, Vol. 4, pp. 473, 524.

42 Kant, *Schriften*, Vol. 4, pp. 508, 511, 512, 515, 516, 534. *Cf.* Gerd Buchdahl, 'Gravity and intelligibility: Newton to Kant', in *The Methodological Heritage of Newton*, ed. R. E. Butts and J. W. Davis (Oxford, 1970), pp. 74–102.

43 Kant, *Schriften*, Vol. 4, p. 543. *Cf.* Buchdahl, *Metaphysics and the Philosophy of Science*, pp. 676–8.

44 Kant, *Schriften*, Vol. 4, pp. 543–4, 549.

45 Kant, *Schriften*, Vol. 4, pp. 549–51.

46 Kant, *Schriften*, Vol. 21, pp. 387, 527.

47 Kant, *Schriften*, Vol. 22, p. 244; *ibid.*, Vol. 21, p. 508.

48 Kant, *Schriften*, Vol. 21, pp. 441–2.

49 Kant, *Schriften*, Vol. 21, pp. 581, 593, 600.

50 Kant, *Schriften*, Vol. 21, pp. 192, 543, 593. *Cf.* W. H. Werkmeister, 'The Critique of Pure Reason and physics', *Kant-Studien*, 68 (1977), 33–45; and Adickes, *Kant als Naturforscher*, Vol. 2, pp. 193–205.

51 B. Tuschling, *Metaphysische und transzendentale Dynamik in Kants opus postumum* (Berlin, 1971), pp. 39–56.

52 Kant, *Schriften*, Vol. 21, p. 381.

53 Kant, *Schriften*, Vol. 21, pp. 225, 444, 576, 600.

54 Kant, *Schriften*, Vol. 21, p. 356.

55 Kant, *Schriften*, Vol. 21, pp. 312–34. *Cf.* Werkmeister, 'The Critique of Pure Reason and physics', pp. 42–5.

56 Kant, *Schriften*, Vol. 21, pp. 288, 593.

CHAPTER V

Faraday: the concept of the physical field

The view now stated of the constitution of matter would seem to involve necessarily the conclusion that matter fills all space, or, at least, all space to which gravitation extends (including the sun and its system); for gravitation is a property of matter dependent on a certain force, and it is this force which constitutes the matter. In that view matter is not merely mutually penetrable, but each atom extends, so to say, throughout the whole of the solar system, yet always retaining its own centre of force. . . . Hence matter will be *continuous* throughout.[1]

§1. Faraday's theory of matter

Faraday's 'Speculation touching electric conduction and the nature of matter' (1844) formulated a theory of matter and the agency of force which aimed to provide a representation of the transmission of forces (gravitational, electrical) in space. In rejecting the philosophical assumptions of atomism Faraday seeks to explain the transmission of force between separated bodies in terms of the spatial disposition of forces. In his 'Speculation on matter' Faraday's concept of the physical 'field', which supposed that forces were mediated by the ambient field between bodies, is grounded on a theory of substance, that force was the defining property of matter. Hence matter filled space by its inherent forces.

In elaborating this metaphysical argument Faraday drew upon a tradition in British natural philosophy which sought to demolish the conceptual foundations of Newtonian atomism. According to this theory of nature, matter was defined in terms of active powers of attraction and repulsion. Forces were conceived as essential to matter and as defining its materiality. Bodies were conceived in terms of collocations of powers, rather than as being composed of particles possessing properties of solidity and impenetrability to which forces were superadded.

In rejecting the basic premises of Newtonian atomism, that impenetrability and extension were essential properties of matter; in replacing the Newtonian dualism of atoms and forces by a monism of force which defined the essence of matter; and in explaining the concept of gravitational attraction in terms of an inherent force diffused through space, Faraday's arguments may seem to echo Kant's discussion of the 'dynamical' explication of matter. The similarities between Faraday and Kant are superficial, as there is no hint of the Kantian application of the categorial principles in Faraday's treatment of matter theory. While there is no evidence of any direct Kantian influence which shaped Faraday's theory of matter, Kant's and Faraday's discussions of matter theory belong to a common tradition of natural philosophy which was concerned to critically reappraise the foundations of Newton's atomism and to explicate the concept of forces acting directly at a distance.

Faraday himself indicated that his theory of matter resembled a theory proposed in R. J. Boscovich's *Theory of Natural Philosophy* (1758),[2] though in fact Boscovich's ideas were quite different from Faraday's concept of matter. Boscovich did not define matter in terms of inherent forces but preserved the Newtonian dualism between force and matter, supposing that matter consisted of nonextended centres from which forces of attraction and repulsion operated. Faraday's theory of matter shows much closer conceptual affinities, and terminological similarities, to arguments advanced by Joseph Priestley in the 1770s.[3] Priestley had maintained that the defining characteristics of matter were extension and inherent forces of attraction and repulsion, rejecting the Newtonian doctrine that impenetrability and solidity were essential properties of matter and affirming a monism of force which defined material substances. Priestley had ambiguously presented his theory as similar to Boscovich's ideas, and while Priestley's arguments were widely disseminated in texts between 1780 and 1830 this theory of matter was customarily designated as Boscovich's theory. Faraday's reference to Boscovich, though misleading, was conventional.

Faraday wrote his 'Speculation on matter' in the course of a reappraisal of his theory of the interaction of electrical forces, and the formulation of this theory of matter initiated a radical reconstruction of his explanation of the propagation of forces and his concept of the physical 'field', a concept which sought to avoid the difficulties of the supposition of forces acting directly between electrified bodies across finite distances of space by supposing that the forces between bodies were mediated by some property of the ambient field or space. The role of Faraday's 'Speculation on matter' in the enunciation of his field theory demonstrates the importance of metaphysical argument and the problem of substance in the development of his theory of the physical field. Faraday's arguments reflect the influence of Priestley and other eighteenth-century British natural philosophers, who sought to critically examine the foundations of Newton's theory of nature. An understanding of the role of metaphysical argument and the problem of substance in shaping Faraday's field theory requires an analysis of this tradition of natural philosophy, and an examination of the place of matter theory in the development of Faraday's theories of electricity.

§2. Faraday's field theory

Faraday first used the term 'magnetic field' in 1845,[4] but he had developed the essential doctrine of the theory of the physical field, the transmission of the action of forces by a mediating agent, in the context of a series of highly original experimental studies in the 1830s. Faraday emphasised the mediation of electrical forces, emphasising the role of a medium surrounding electrified bodies in transmitting electrical forces. Faraday supposed that the particles of this mediating substance were subjected to a 'state of tension' by the electric force, an 'electrical condition of matter' which he termed the 'electrotonic state'. He explained this state of electrical tension in terms of the polarisation of the molecules of the mediating substance, by which he meant a disposition of force by which a molecule acquired opposite electrical 'powers', positive and negative electrical charges, on different parts.

In a major study of the agency of electric charges in 1837 Faraday demonstrated that the induction of electric charges between bodies took place along curved lines, a phenomenon which he explained in terms of the transmission of forces by the particles of a mediating substance, which he termed the 'dielectric' medium; he claimed that electrostatic induction was mediated by the transmission of force between the polarised particles of a 'dielectric' medium surrounding the electrified bodies. He also demonstrated experimentally that different substances had different capacities for the transmission of electrostatic forces, a phenomenon which indicated the mediating role of the dielectric medium.[5]

The kernel of Faraday's field theory was therefore the representation of the transmission of force by the mediation of the ambient field, and he emphasises that in a field represented by the agency of the particles of the space-pervading dielectric, the particles which mediate the action of the field only act on neighbouring particles. He declares that he considers the induction of electrostatic forces to be caused by 'an action of contiguous particles consisting in a species of polarity' and that 'electrical action at a distance . . . never occurred except through the influence of the intervening matter' of the dielectric.

Faraday does not however conceive the particles of the dielectric to be polarised as a result of mutual contact. In seeking to clarify his argument he observes that 'I mean by contiguous particles those which are next to each other, not that there is *no* space between them'. The polarised particles of the dielectric do not transmit forces by contact action, but by the agency of their polarised forces. Faraday therefore rejects both action at a distance and the mediation of force by the contact action of the particles of the dielectric. While Faraday's concept of the transmission of force between contiguous polarised particles provided no explanation of the mechanism by which the forces were propagated, he implies that electrical forces were manifested in the space surrounding the electrically polarised particles of the dielectric medium, and that electrical action was to be explained in terms of the agency of the '*contiguous* [neighbouring] and intermediate particles' of the dielectric.[6]

In response to criticism of his conception of the interaction of the forces between the polarised particles of the dielectric medium,[7] Faraday sought to clarify the connection between the nature of matter and the agency of force. He had placed the focus of his argument on a theory of electrical action grounded on the concept of the polarity of the particles of the dielectric, rather than on the discussion of the relationship between the particles of the dielectric medium and their associated forces. His 'Speculation touching electric conduction and the nature of matter' (1844) provided a reappraisal of the relationship between matter and force which aimed to establish the intelligibility of Faraday's denial of action at a distance. He points out that, according to the atomic theory of matter, atoms were not considered as being in contact, and hence if action between contiguous particles was denied then it would be necessary to ascribe a role to the intermediate spaces between the atoms to account for the communication of forces between particles. In Faraday's view void space could not have causal or dispositional properties analogous to the active powers associated with material substances; as he later emphasised, 'mere space cannot act as matter acts'.[8] The agency of the interatomic void was therefore inconceivable, and he concludes that the theory of atoms and void space should be rejected.

Faraday goes on to argue that all knowledge of matter was limited to ideas of the 'system of powers or forces in and around' material substances, and he asserts that matter should not be envisaged as consisting of extended, impenetrable atoms surrounded by forces of attraction and repulsion, but that matter should be represented as a plenum of 'powers'. He declares that 'the substance consists of the powers', maintaining that it was impossible to conceive '*matter* independent of the powers'. According to this theory 'particles of matter' were in reality 'centres of force'. This theory of matter resolved the problem of explaining the mode of the transmission of electrical forces, for 'matter will be *continuous* throughout, and in considering a mass of it we have not to suppose a distinction between its atoms and any intervening space'. By virtue of its 'forces' or 'powers' matter was envisaged as a continuum, and the interaction between matter and force was explicated in terms of the definition of matter as a plenum of force, being envisaged as interactions between 'centres of force' or collocations of 'powers' diffused through space.

In affirming that forces 'constitute the matter' Faraday rejected the Newtonian doctrine that extension and impenetrability were essential, absolute properties defining material substances. Faraday affirms the 'mutual penetrability of matter', for in terms of the theory of matter as constituted of forces, the interaction between material substances 'will depend upon the relative disposition of the powers', and matter *qua* 'centres of power' will therefore 'mutually penetrate to the very centres', like the 'conjunction of two sea waves of different velocities into one'. Faraday's theory of matter thus established impenetrability as a derivative property of matter, admitting of degrees of intensity, and dependent upon the disposition of the forces which define matter. The interaction of electrified bodies is therefore envisaged in terms of the disposition and coalescence of the intensive forces which constitute matter; action between electrified bodies is explained by the theory that 'matter fills all space' while 'always retaining its own centre of force'.[9]

The formulation of this theory of matter as constituted of inherent forces led Faraday to reconstruct his theory of the physical field. In his 'Thoughts on ray-vibrations' (1846) he states that the theory of matter as a collocation of forces had led him to consider that the propagation of forces could be represented in terms of vibrations in 'lines of force'. In the 1830s he had employed the concept of 'lines of force' merely·to represent the alignment of the polarised particles of the dielectric, as a 'temporary conventional mode of expressing the direction of the power' of electrical forces.[10] He now argues that in conceiving matter as force diffused through space, the concept of lines of force represented the disposition of material substances in space. He declares that 'the particle indeed is supposed to exist only by these forces, and where they are it is'.[11] The interaction between material substances was to be represented in terms of the lines of force which permeated space. This led Faraday to abandon the concept of the polarisation of the particles of the dielectric, represented by the electro-tonic state, in favour of a theory of the primacy of lines of force. He now used the term 'polarity' merely to represent the direction of the lines of force in the field of forces, not the polarisation of particles.

Faraday developed this theory in a series of experimental papers on magnetism. He detected the rotational effect of magnetic forces on polarised light, explaining this phenomenon in terms of the agency of the lines of magnetic force. He explained the differences in the magnetic character of different substances in terms of the propensity of lines of force to pass through them. He summarised his new conceptual framework in a paper on 'The physical character of the lines of magnetic force' (1852). He declared that electric and magnetic lines of force had a real physical existence, maintaining that the forces 'can only have relation to each other by *curved* lines of force through the surrounding space; and I cannot conceive curved lines of force without the conditions of a physical existence in that intermediate space'.

The lines of force were now conceived as the primary entities representing physical reality, rather than mere symbols which expressed the alignment of polarised particles. He emphasised his changed interpretation of the physical structure of the field, observing that the concept of the electro-tonic state 'would coincide and become identified with that which would then constitute the physical lines of magnetic force'. The tension and polarisation of particles were replaced by the concept of the primacy of lines of force, a theory of the physical field which was grounded on Faraday's theory of matter as constituted of forces.[12]

Faraday endeavoured to extend this theory of the field to explain the phenomenon of gravitational attraction. He argues that lines of gravitational force spread out through space so that 'the power is always existing around the sun and through infinite space, whether secondary bodies be there to be acted upon by gravitation or not; and not only around the sun, but around every particle of matter which has existence'.[13] As he had argued in his 'Speculation on matter', matter fills all space by its forces, and gravitation could therefore be explained as a property of matter envisaged as a collocation of forces, an interpretation which he sought to illustrate by reference to the theory of the primacy of lines of force in space, a field theory of gravitation.

Faraday therefore introduced two distinct representations of the physical field, in terms of the mediation by the particles of an ambient medium, and in terms of a plenum of force represented by the concept of the primacy of lines of force. These two formulations, envisaged as distinct alternative physical modes of representation of the field by Faraday, shaped the subsequent development of the field concept. Neither theory of Faraday's provided an explanation of the mechanism by which forces were propagated in the field, and this problem dominated the work of Faraday's successors. Maxwell attempted to develop a physical theory of the propagation of forces in the field by appeal to the concept of a particular ether, and he also adopted Faraday's concept of lines of force as a means of representing the field. Nevertheless Maxwell did not accept Faraday's physical interpretation of lines of force as grounded on the concept of matter as filling space by its inherent forces. Maxwell observed that Faraday 'even speaks of the lines of force belonging to a body as in some sense part of itself', but he denied that the notion of lines of force defining the material substance of bodies should be construed as essential to Faraday's theory of the field.[14] For Maxwell, the theory of lines of force represented the spatial distribution of forces; while for Faraday, the concept of the primacy of lines of force was grounded on the theory of substance expounded in his 'Speculation on matter'.

For Faraday, the theory of lines of force was not simply to be construed as a 'functional' model for the representation of the spatial distribution and intensity of forces in the field. The problem of substance was fundamental to Faraday's formulation of field theory, and the ontological primacy of lines of force was rendered intelligible by Faraday's metaphysical explication of matter as constituted of inherent forces. Faraday's appeal to metaphysical argument in seeking to clarify the relation between matter and force highlights the centrality of the metaphysical problems of matter theory in the development of the field concept. The framework of Faraday's metaphysics of matter, the doctrine that the essence of matter is constituted of inherent 'powers' or 'forces', contrasts with the philosophical assumption of atomism, grounded on Newton's doctrine of essential qualities and the distinction between primary and secondary qualities. Faraday's arguments on the metaphysics of matter theory echo the critiques of Newtonian atomism which were current in eighteenth-century British natural philosophy, and an understanding of the framework of Faraday's metaphysical arguments requires an analysis of this tradition.

§3. The concept of causal powers

The doctrine of primary and secondary qualities was a central feature of the discussion of matter theory in the writings of seventeenth-century philosophers and natural philosophers. Boyle and Locke were concerned to establish a distinction between essential or absolute and relational qualities of matter. They argued that the essential or primary characteristics of matter, such as spatial extension and solidity, existed independently of human perception; while secondary qualities, such as sound and colour, were held to arise as a result of a relation between the perceiving mind and the primary qualities of matter which provided their causal nexus. Primary properties of matter were therefore intrinsic to the nature of material substances, while secondary qualities were derivative and relational.

Boyle argued that all changes in observable matter arose from changes in the constituent unobservable corpuscles of matter. In his *Origine of Formes and Qualities* (1666) Boyle emphasised that the primary properties of size, shape and motion were the essential and universal properties of matter, and were absolute and nonrelational qualities. In his *Essay Concerning Human Understanding* (1690) Locke declared that the 'primary' qualities of bodies are 'utterly inseparable' from the essential nature of matter. These 'original' qualities, solidity, extension, figure and motion, are essential properties of body, and Locke distinguishes them from 'secondary' qualities which 'are nothing in the objects themselves', and which are produced as an effect of the primary qualities and hence are relational. Locke maintains that besides the original or primary properties matter possesses dispositional or relational properties, which he terms causal 'powers'.[15]

Boyle had also drawn a distinction between the essential properties which were inherent in bodies and relational properties, arguing that a body had a 'disposition of its constituent Corpuscles' to produce sensations of colour and sound, while being endowed '*actually* but onely with those more Catholick [universal] Affections of Bodies, Figure, Motion, Texture, etc'.[16] Locke argues that unlike primary qualities, which have the power to produce ideas of extension and motion in our awareness and which are also essential properties of matter, properties of colour, sound and taste are 'powers barely, and nothing but powers' which 'result from the different modifications of those primary qualities'. Sensible qualities which are merely powers that bodies have to affect our senses, such as colours and sounds, are therefore categorically distinguished from the primary qualities, which (though they are also sensible qualities) are conceived as nonrelational and inherent properties of matter.[17] The distinction between those sensible qualities which are defining characteristics of matter and properties which are causal powers emphasises the intrinsic passivity of material entities; the primary properties of matter are the passive properties of extension, solidity and motion. Locke denies that bodies possess inherent activity such as an 'active power to move'. Bodies are therefore inherently passive.[18]

In rejecting the atomistic assumptions of Boyle, Locke and Newton natural philosophers such as Priestley argued that causal powers were substantively present in material entities. The essence of matter was defined in terms of inherent active 'powers' rather than the extension and solidity of the primordial corpuscles of matter. This definition of matter in terms of inherent active powers was grounded on the rejection of Locke's disjunction between absolute and relational properties, an issue which received a sustained analysis in the work of Berkeley and Hume. In his *Principles of Human Knowledge* (1710) Berkeley rejects the theory of a substratum of invisible particles; whatever its utility as an explanatory scheme, the supposition of atoms could not be justified by philosophical analysis. All that is known of external reality is what is perceivable, and all the sensible qualities of bodies are relational: 'extension, figure, and motion, abstracted from all other qualities, are inconceivable'.[19] All the qualities of bodies have the same ontological status, and there is no justification for the ascription of absolute or primary qualities to the putative particles of the corpuscular philosophy.

In his *Treatise of Human Nature* (1739) Hume presents a devastating critique of the metaphysical assumptions of atomism, arguing that there is no epistemological basis for the distinction between primary and secondary qualities. Having accepted that qualities such as colours and tastes are relational, then it follows that all the qualities of bodies are relational. The primary qualities of matter are therefore reduced to the perceptible domain of secondary qualities, and we have 'no just nor satisfactory idea of solidity' as an absolute quality defining the essence of matter. Hence there 'remains nothing, which can afford us a just and consistent idea of body'.[20] Moreover, Hume denies the thesis that the 'power and efficacy' of matter defines the essence of matter, for 'we never have any impression, that contains any power or efficacy'. Nevertheless, as he explains in his *Enquiry into the Human Understanding* (1748), the notion that matter has a real power can be made intelligible if this power can be shown to be an instance of causal activity. Hence, subsuming the phenomenon of gravity under the agency of Newton's 'etherial active fluid' renders the concept of a gravitational attractive force intelligible. For Hume the concept of active 'power' cannot be conceived as a defining property of matter, but can be employed in physical explanations, to explicate the laws of nature between material entities.[21]

In restricting the intelligibility of causal explanation to the formulation of physical laws Hume rejected the notion of the efficient causality of divine agency sustaining the natural world. Hume's restriction of the causal principle to the formulation of physical explanations was resisted by the Scottish philosopher Thomas Reid, and in his *Essays on the Active Powers of the Human Mind* (1788) Reid attempted to provide a systematic refutation of Hume's theory of causality. Reid distinguishes between causation in the sense of the formulation of laws of nature, which was the concern of science and which Hume accepted as a valid explication of causality, and 'efficient causation', as in divine sustenance of the laws of nature. Reid argues that natural philosophers were merely concerned with laws of nature which were 'the rules according to which the effects are produced'; nevertheless it was intelligible to suppose the operation of efficient causes in nature even though the mind can never know 'what their nature, their number, and their different offices may be', for natural effects cannot be produced simply by rules. Reid thus seeks to justify the supposition that the activity of nature was a consequence of divine causality, and that concepts of *cause, agency* and *active power* could be employed in characterising the operations of nature.

The thrust of Reid's argument is therefore to render intelligible the concept of the 'active powers which philosophers teach us to ascribe to matter', powers such as gravitational attraction. While the nature of these active powers and their relation to divine agency remained obscure, Reid provides a justification of the ascription of active powers to matter.[22]

§4. Ether and the activity of matter

Reid's justification of the concept of active powers reflects a transformation in eighteenth-century British natural philosophy, involving the rejection of Newton's doctrine of the intrinsic passivity of matter and the transformation of Newton's concept of active principles. By the 1740s natural philosophers had developed conceptions of nature in which the ether was envisaged as an active principle which was immanent in the fabric of nature, and which functioned as the source of the activity of nature. This transformation in the concept of nature involved a blurring of the distinctive categories of Newton's natural philosophy and a rejection of its theological foundations. In Newton's natural philosophy active principles were conceived as distinct from the passive properties of matter and as the manifestation of God's causal agency in nature. The ambiguous conceptual status of the ether of the 1717 *Opticks* as both an active and a material principle led many theorists to interpret ether as a substance endowed with inherent activity, thus conflating the active-passive dualism of Newton's natural philosophy.

Newton's theory of the ether had aroused little interest among natural philosphers until the 1740s. Newtonian natural philosophers had emphasised Newton's theory of the attractive force of gravity and his theological argument in explaining gravity as the effect of divine agency, and had sought to elaborate Newton's theory of short-range interparticulate forces as developed in the queries to the *Opticks* rather than the theory of the ether. The interest in the experimental effects of electricity led in the 1740s to a new concern with Newton's ether, fostered by the publication of some of Newton's early speculations on ether. It was argued that while Newton had placed little emphasis on the theory of ether, contemporary natural philosophers 'can now almost prove the existence of this aether by the phenomena of electricity'.[23]

The increasing stress on the role of repulsive forces by natural philosophers, and the impact of Boerhaave's concept of 'fire', fostered this shift in opinion. While the early Newtonians had stressed the importance of attractive forces in explaining the phenomena of chemistry, in his *Vegetable Staticks* (1727) Stephen Hales developed the implications of Newton's discussion in the *Opticks* of the role of repulsive forces in determining the properties of gases. Newton had argued that gases, like the ether, contained particles endowed with repulsive forces, and Hales sought to explain chemical processes in terms of the interaction between the repellent particles of gases and the attractive forces of ordinary matter. Hales supposed a balance in nature between attracting matter and the repelling particles of gases, arguing that nature was inherently active, its activity maintained by the 'incessant action' of attractive and repulsive forces.[24]

Herman Boerhaave's *New Method of Chemistry* (1732) emphasised the role of 'fire' in maintaining the activity of the universe, for through the agency of the 'active element' of fire 'the whole universe might continue in perpetual motion'.[25] As a substance possessing inherent activity fire came to be interpreted as being analogous to Newton's ether, an active principle maintaining the activity of nature. The conflation of ether-fire as an inherently active substance, and Boerhaave's theory of a dualism in nature between fire and the attractive forces of ordinary matter, led natural philosophers to develop dualistic theories in which 'elementary fire' was considered to be an ethereal substance 'endowed with active powers distinct from those of other matter'.[26] Boerhaave's ethereal fire, Hales' dualism of ordinary matter surrounded by repelling ethereal particles of gases, and Newton's theory of the ether shaped the influential theory of electrification proposed by Benjamin Franklin in the late 1740s, based on a dualism of ordinary matter and the repulsive particles of an electric ethereal substance. In the writings of natural philosophers the phenomenon of electricity led to the assertion of the identity of fire, electricity and ether, and to the interpretation of the ether as a repelling, inherently active, material substance.[27]

In the natural philosophy of the 1740s Newton's concept of ether as an active principle was transformed. The ambiguous conceptual status of Newton's ether as both an active principle and a material substance, and the conflation of ether-fire as an inherently active substance, led to the interpretation of ether as an inherently active substance endowed with repulsive force. Newton's dualism between active principles and the passive principles of matter was conflated; the active powers of the ether were conceived as intrinsic to its materiality. The conflation of the Newtonian dualism between active and passive principles, the enunciation of a conception of nature in terms of a balance between attractive and repulsive forces, associated respectively with ordinary matter and with ethereal fire or electricity, led to the development of the view that ether was an inherently active substance endowed with repulsive force and that ordinary matter was to be considered as possessing an inherent attractive force. This theory contradicted Newton's concept of the intrinsic passivity of material entities, for all activity was subsumed in the inherent powers of material substances. Newton's theological explication of gravity as the effect of divine agency was rejected. Motion was viewed as inherent in matter, and nature was conceived in terms of immanent active powers.[28]

In the second half of the eighteenth century this theory of the ether as an inherently active substance endowed with repulsive force was elaborated into a unified ether theory. The ethereal 'electrical fire' and 'phlogiston' (the chemical principle of inflammability) were envisaged as different 'modifications' of a universal, inherently active ether. Thermal, electrical and chemical phenomena were explained in terms of the ether, and these physical phenomena were reduced to the interaction of attractive and repulsive forces, to a dualism of ordinary matter and ether in its different modifications. The 'balance' of the active 'powers' of attraction and repulsion maintained the order of nature; the operations of the 'ethereal matter' of fire, electricity and phlogiston activated the cosmos.[29] Newton's disjunction between active principles and passive matter was abandoned in favour of a theory of nature in which matter endowed with attractive force balanced the ethereal substance endowed with inherent repulsive force, a conception of nature grounded on the intrinsic activity of matter. Active powers were immanent in matter.

§5. Priestley's theory of matter

In his *Disquisitions Relating to Matter and Spirit* (1777) Joseph Priestley rejected the Newtonian duality of active and passive principles because of the difficulty in explaining God's causal relation to nature entailed by supposing that God 'has no property whatever in common with matter'. This would imply that 'the divine being is necessarily cut off from all communication with, and all action and influence upon, his own creation'.[30] Priestley sought to resolve the problem of the interaction between matter and divine agency by positing a monistic theory of nature, denying the Newtonian dualism of matter and force by defining matter in terms of inherent powers of attraction and repulsion. Priestley rejects the separate categories of matter and spirit, contesting the atomistic theory of substance in which matter was 'said to be possessed of the property of extension' and also of 'solidity or impenetrability', but was 'said to be naturally destitute of all powers whatever'. By contrast, spirit was defined as an immaterial substance which was endowed with inherent powers and activity. According to this dualistic ontology, he claims, the connection and interaction of matter and spirit could not be explained. In Priestley's view matter and spirit could not interact unless they had common properties. He therefore concludes that 'matter is not that inert substance that it has been supposed to be; that powers of attraction or repulsion are necessary to its very being, and that no part of it appears to be impenetrable to other parts'.[31]

Priestley's rejection of a dualistic ontology is based on a critique of the doctrine that solidity and impenetrability are essential or primary properties of matter. He denies that the experience of the senses establishes solidity and impenetrability as absolute, nonrelational and essential properties of matter. The absolute existence of primary qualities like solidity and impenetrability is not established by sensory experience, for our experience of bodies only provided evidence that matter was endowed with resisting powers. Priestley argues that 'resistance, on which alone our opinion concerning the solidity or impenetrability of matter is founded, is never occasioned by solid matter, but by . . . a power of repulsion'. All that can be gathered about external reality from tactile experience is that the 'resistance [of bodies] can differ only in degree'. From this Priestley concludes that bodies possess a 'greater or less repulsive power', and maintains that there is no evidence for the 'supposition of a cause of resistance entirely different from such a power'.

There was therefore no evidence that the cause of the resisting power of bodies was to be grounded in the solidity and impenetrability of the component particles of bodies. While the atomistic ontology assumed that there was an invisible substratum of particles beyond the experience of the senses, and that these particles possessed the primary properties of solidity and impenetrability, Priestley maintains that 'we know nothing more of the nature of substance than it is something which supports properties' of attraction and repulsion.[32] Solidity was not an absolute and nonrelational property of matter, for solidity and impenetrability were mere effects of the powers of attraction and repulsion. Solidity 'could not be deduced from sense, but must have its origin in the understanding'.[33]

In contesting Locke's doctrine of primary qualities Priestley argues that matter could not be defined other than in terms of its powers of attraction and repulsion. He defines matter as 'a substance possessed of the property of extension, and of powers of attraction or repulsion'. These powers were conceived to exist in a substantive sense, and not merely relationally or dispositionally as in Locke's theory of causal powers. The apparent impenetrability and solidity of matter were not essential properties of matter; resistance was not due to the solidity and impenetrability of the particles of matter but to an inherent power of repulsion. The powers were 'essential to the *actual existence* of all matter'. Hence Priestley concludes that 'whatever solidity any body has, it is possessed of it only in consequence of being endued with certain *powers*'.[34] Active powers define the essence of matter, and he declares that 'take away attraction and repulsion, and matter vanishes'. These powers are therefore 'essential to the being of matter, and without which it cannot exist as a material substance'. Nevertheless he did not explain the way in which powers could 'inhere in' or 'belong to' matter; the powers of attraction and repulsion were fundamental properties which by their action gave the appearance of solidity to matter.

Matter was therefore conceived as a complex of intensive powers, and the resistance of matter to penetration by other matter was dependent on the degree of resistance manifested by the repulsive powers of material substances. Priestley, like Faraday later, thus asserts the 'mutual penetrability of matter'. Impenetrability is not an absolute property of matter; the resistance of matter to penetration admits of degrees of intensity, and hence the penetrability of matter is relational, being dependent on the active powers defining the nature of material substances.[35]

In contesting the philosophical foundations of atomism Priestley seeks to provide a metaphysical reappraisal of the relation between the concepts of matter and force. Priestley rejects Newton's dualism of matter and force, the concept of matter as a passive entity resisting change while force was conceived as an external agent generating change. In Priestley's view this theory of nature not only could not explain divine agency in nature, but also was based on false philosophical premises, the doctrine of primary or essential qualities. The thrust of Priestley's metaphysical argument is to establish the intelligibility of the concept of force by explicating a monistic theory of nature, in which matter is defined as a penetrable substance endowed with active powers of attraction and repulsion. Rejecting the metaphysical foundations of Newton's physics, Priestley seeks to ground the concept of force in terms of a theory of substance in which forces of attraction and repulsion are construed as intrinsic to matter. Priestley's justification of the intelligibility of the concept of force is thus based on a metaphysical explication of the concept of substance.

§6. Hutton's theory of powers

James Hutton's *Dissertations on Different Subjects in Natural Philosophy* (1792) and his *Investigation of the Principles of Knowledge* (1794), though less well-known than his geological writings, provide important discussions of the concept of substance as active powers. Like Priestley, Hutton rejects atomism and with it the doctrine of primary qualities. He emphasises that according to the principles of Newtonian atomism 'it is believed that every material substance has necessarily a certain volume, which fundamentally is unalterable'. Hence solidity 'must appear to be the proper idea of substance in that philosophy'. This is Newton's view that bodies fill or occupy space in an absolute sense, and it is this doctrine which Hutton rejects as untenable. He declares that properties such as 'magnitude and figure [the defining characteristics of atoms] have no other existence than in the conceiving faculty of our mind'. These properties were not absolute properties of substance but were 'truly ideas formed upon certain occasions'.[36] Sensory experience, far from providing knowledge of extended, hard matter, only gave us evidence of 'resisting powers in bodies, by which their volume and figure are presented to us'.

Hutton therefore rejects the 'received opinion of philosophers', that 'matter, of which natural bodies are composed, is perfectly hard and impenetrable'. Qualities of bodies such as extension and impenetrability are only 'conditional', depending on the contraction or dilation of the intensive powers from which they arise. Hence properties like extension and solidity do not 'arise from the absolute nature' of matter possessing essential qualities of extension and solidity, since these properties are relational, and can be modified by the disposition of the intensive powers characterising matter.[37] Hutton therefore firmly opposes the Newtonian doctrine that 'bodies are composed of atoms which are absolutely inert . . . infinitely hard, and perfectly incompressible'.[38]

The extension and solidity of bodies are therefore sensible properties of bodies, but these properties should not be construed as absolute, nonrelational and essential properties of matter. While we perceive gross bodies as possessing the properties of extension and solidity, these properties are the effects of intensive powers. Moreover, the nature of 'matter', the 'substance, essence, or principles of external things', cannot be explicated in terms of observable properties of bodies. To assume that material substance was composed of extended, solid, hard atoms would be to assume as the principles of bodies 'nothing but the bodies themselves under the pedantic designation of atoms or corpuscles'.[39] Hutton therefore implicitly denies Newton's third rule of philosophising, the 'analogy of nature' which justified the ascription of observable and essential properties of extension and solidity as universal properties of matter, as the essential properties of unobservable atoms. Hutton concludes that 'matter . . . will appear to be a thing absolutely different from that external thing which is perceived by our mind'.[40] The ultimate nature of matter therefore remains obscure: 'we never shall learn to known what matter is in itself'. Nevertheless 'whatever matter is of itself, it must be considered as the cause of motion and resistance in natural bodies'.[41]

Hutton declares that 'power, the cause of our sensation, is to be considered as a first cause', and it is from our knowledge of intensive powers that we are to infer the characteristics of the nature of material substance. Hutton concludes that activity is an essential property of substances, and asserts that 'instead of considering matter as a thing inert, and only passive in its nature . . . we find it necessary to conceive power of action to exist in external things'. He declares that 'matter [is] thus conceived as having power or efficacy'.[42] Though our knowledge of the nature of matter is necessarily imperfect, given the epistemological gap between our perceptions of gross bodies and the characteristics of the unobservable substratum, the 'resisting powers' of bodies provide the sole evidence upon which we can infer the nature of matter.

Hutton's discussion of the 'metaphysical idea of matter' seeks to clarify the metaphysical foundations of natural philosophy. The explication of matter in terms of intensive powers clarifies the relationship between force and inertia. While the forces of attraction and repulsion are grounded on the 'acting powers' which define the nature of material substance, the property of inertia is a passive property of gross bodies not a property of the underlying substratum of 'matter'. He emphasises that 'it is not in the *matter*, which constitutes natural bodies, that the law of *inertia* has been investigated, but in the bodies themselves'. Thus 'there is not any evidence of *inertia* being proper to the matter'. The property of inertia is not an absolute property of material substance but is derivative, being dependent on the intensive powers which characterise matter. He argues that bodies 'acquire inertia in the balance of those opposite powers' of attraction and repulsion.[43]

Hutton thus provides a metaphysical justification of the intelligibility of the concepts of force and inertia in terms of his theory of substance. The disjunction between force and inertia is explicated in terms of the theory of matter as active powers, and Hutton contests the Newtonian doctrine of inertia as an essential property of matter. In Hutton's natural philosophy, inertia is a passive principle of bodies and hence is a relational property of the active powers which characterise substances. On the theological level, this conception of nature contrasts with Newton's stress on divine sustenance by means of active principles, for in Hutton's natural philosophy activity is subsumed in the active powers constituting material substances. Nature is conceived in terms of a balance between powers of attraction and repulsion; as a self-regenerating system of active powers, the self-sufficiency of nature is maintained by the inherent activity of matter. Hutton thus provides a systematic discussion of the theory of matter as constituted of active powers, seeking to clarify the relation between concepts of matter and force.

§7. Forces and fields

The work of Priestley and Hutton provided important critiques of the metaphysical foundations of Newton's physics, based on a rejection of the Newtonian concept of substance. The theory of matter and its associated concepts of activity and passivity, the status of the properties of solidity and impenetrability, and the relation between force, matter and inertia, provided the focus for these discussions. In rejecting Newtonian atomism and in defining matter in terms of inherent forces or 'powers', these arguments display clear conceptual similarities to Faraday's discussion of the nature of substance in his 1844 'Speculation touching electric conduction and the nature of matter'. The overall thrust of Faraday's argument, that matter was to be defined in terms of inherent powers and that matter was therefore penetrable, the impenetrability of substances being relational and dependent on the powers constituting material substances, suggests the influence of eighteenth-century discussions of matter theory. The focus of these discussions, in criticising the metaphysical assumptions underlying the theory of atomism, highlights the importance of Faraday's reappraisal of the nature of substance in the formulation of his theory of the physical field. The similarity of Faraday's arguments to those of Priestley is especially striking, and no doubt reflects the wide discussion of Priestley's account of matter theory between 1780 and 1830.[44]

The feature of the 1844 'Speculation on matter' which was most crucial for Faraday's theory of the field, conceived in terms of physical lines of force diffused through space, was his claim that the theory of matter as defined by inherent forces could explain the interaction of matter and force. If 'particles of matter' were in reality 'centres of force' then 'matter fills all space' while 'always retaining its own centre of force'.[45] The problem of action at a distance could therefore be explicated in terms of a theory of forces permeating space, a theory which was grounded on the abandonment of Newton's concept of substance.

A similar argument to Faraday's was developed by John Playfair in the course of an extended account of Hutton's natural philosophy. Hutton's work and Playfair's discussion were quite likely unknown to Faraday, yet Playfair's argument, which also shows similarities to Kant's treatment of the problem of action at a distance, has interesting parallels to Faraday's later argument. Playfair declared that:

> If it be true that in the material world every phenomenon can be explained by the existence of power, the supposition of extended particles as a *substratum* or residence for such power, is a mere hypothesis, without any countenance from the matter of fact. For if these solid particles are never in contact with one another, what part can they have in the production of

natural appearances, or in what sense can they be called the residence of a force which never acts at the point where they are present? Such particles, therefore, ought to be entirely discarded from any theory that proposes to explain the phenomena of the material world. Thus it appears, that power is the essence of matter, and that none of our perceptions warrant us in considering even body as involving anything more than force, subjected to various laws and combinations.

Playfair went on to state that matter conceived in this way was 'indefinitely extended' through all space 'as is proved by the universality of gravitation'. He emphasised that according to Hutton's system gravitation was not to be construed as 'the action of two distant bodies upon one another, but it is the action of certain powers, diffused through all space, which may be transmitted to any distance'.[46]

These passages establish a clear conceptual link between the reformulation of the definition of matter in terms of intensive powers and the interaction of matter and force as conceived by Faraday, providing the ontological basis of his concept of the physical field: 'each atoms extends, so to say, throughout the whole of the solar system', for 'matter fills all space, or, at least, all space to which gravitation extends'.[47]

Notes

[1] Michael Faraday, 'A speculation touching electric conduction and the nature of matter' [1844], *Experimental Researches in Electricity*, 3 vols. (London, 1839–55), Vol. 2, pp. 291–3.

[2] Faraday, *Electricity*, Vol. 2, p. 290. On the work of Boscovich, with a claim for its extensive influence on Faraday, see L. P. Williams, *Michael Faraday* (London, 1965). *Cf.* J. B. Spencer, 'Boscovich's theory and its relation to Faraday's researches: an analytic approach', *Arch. Hist. Exact Sci.*, 4 (1967), 184–202.

[3] P. M. Heimann, 'Faraday's theories of matter and electricity', *Brit. J. Hist. Sci.*, 5 (1971), 235–57.

[4] Faraday, *Electricity*, Vol. 3, p. 30.

[5] Faraday, *Electricity*, Vol. 1, pp. 16, 19, 411, 393.

[6] Faraday, *Electricity*, Vol. 1, pp. 362, 531, 514. *Cf.* D. C. Gooding, 'Conceptual and experimental bases of Faraday's denial of electrostatic action at a distance', *Stud. Hist. Phil. Sci.*, 9 (1978), 117–49. On the context of Faraday's work see J. L. Heilbron, 'The electric field before Faraday', in *Conceptions of Ether*, ed. G. N. Cantor and M. J. S. Hodge (Cambridge, 1981), pp. 187–213.

[7] R. Hare, 'A letter to Professor Faraday' and M. Faraday, 'An answer to Dr. Hare's letter' [1840], *Electricity*, Vol. 2, pp. 251–74.

8 Faraday, *Electricity*, Vol. 3, p. 194.

9 Faraday, *Electricity*, Vol. 2, pp. 289–93.

10 Faraday, *Electricity*, Vol. 1, p. 386.

11 M. Faraday, 'Thoughts on ray-vibrations' [1846], *Electricity*, Vol. 3, p. 447.

12 M. Faraday, 'On the physical character of the lines of magnetic force' [1852], *Electricity*, Vol. 3, pp. 414, 420–1.

13 Faraday, *Electricity*, Vol. 3, p. 574.

14 J. C. Maxwell, *A Treatise on Electricity and Magnetism*, 2 vols. (Oxford, 1873), Vol. 2, p. 164.

15 John Locke, *An Essay Concerning Human Understanding* [1690], ed. A. S. Pringle-Pattison (Oxford, 1924), pp. 66–7. On primary and secondary qualities see M. Mandelbaum, *Philosophy, Science and Sense Perception* (Baltimore, 1964).

16 Robert Boyle, *The Origine of Formes and Qualities* (Oxford, 1666), pp. 47–9.

17 Locke, *Essay*, p. 72. *Cf.* J. W. Yolton, *Locke and the Compass of Human Understanding* (Cambridge, 1970), pp. 21–5.

18 Locke, *Essay*, p. 138. *Cf.* R. M. Mattern, 'Locke on active power and the obscure idea of active power from bodies', *Stud. Hist. Phil. Sci.*, 11 (1980), 39–77.

19 George Berkeley, *The Principles of Human Knowledge* [1710], *The Works of George Berkeley*, 9 vols., ed. A. A. Luce and T. E. Jessop (London, 1948–57), Vol. 2, p. 45. *Cf.* G. Buchdahl, *Metaphysics and the Philosophy of Science* (Oxford, 1969), pp. 307–17.

20 David Hume, *A Treatise of Human Nature* [1739], ed. L. A. Selby-Bigge (Oxford, 1888), p. 229.

21 Hume, *Treatise*, pp. 160–1; *idem*, *An Enquiry into the Human Understanding* [1748], ed. L. A. Selby-Bigge (Oxford, 1902), p. 73 n. See also Buchdahl, *Metaphysics and the Philosophy of Science*, pp. 325–87.

22 Thomas Reid, *Essays on the Active Powers of the Human Mind* [1788], ed. B. Brody (Cambridge, Mass., 1969), pp. 40, 46, 47. See P. M. Heimann and J. E. McGuire, 'Newtonian forces and Lockean powers: concepts of matter in eighteenth-century thought', *Hist. Stud. Phys. Sci.*, 3 (1971), 261–8.

23 Benjamin Martin, *Philosophia Britannica* [1747], quoted in A. Thackray, *Atoms and Powers* (Cambridge, Mass., 1970), p. 135.

24 S. Hales, *Vegetable Staticks* (London, 1727), p. 178.

25 H. Boerhaave, *A New Method of Chemistry*, trans. P. Shaw, 2 vols. (London, 1741), Vol. 1, pp. 212, 362.

26 J. Rowning, *A Compendious System of Natural Philosophy* (London, 1737–43), p. iii.

27 P. M. Heimann, 'Ether and imponderables', in *Conceptions of Ether*, ed. G. N. Cantor and M. J. S. Hodge (Cambridge, 1981), pp. 61–83.

28 *Cf.* Heimann and McGuire, 'Newtonian forces and Lockean powers', pp. 296–304.

29 A. Walker, *A System of Familiar Philosophy*, rev. ed., 2 vols. (London, 1802), Vol. 1, pp. 6, 14, 18.

30 Joseph Priestley, *Disquisitions Relating to Matter and Spirit* [2nd ed., 1782],

The Theological and Miscellaneous Works of Joseph Priestley. 25 vols., ed. J. T. Rutt (London, 1817–31), Vol. 3, p. 298.

31 Priestley, *Works*, Vol. 3. pp. 218–19.

32 Priestley, *Works*, Vol. 3, pp. 223, 227. See Heimann and McGuire, 'Newtonian forces and Lockean powers', pp. 268–81.

33 J. Priestley, *Hartley's Theory of the Human Mind* [1775], *Works*, Vol. 3, p. 191.

34 Priestley, [*Disquisitions*,] *Works*, Vol. 3, pp. 219, 223, 225.

35 Priestley, *Works*, Vol. 3, p. 224, 232, 238.

36 James Hutton, *An Investigation of the Principles of Knowledge*, 3 vols. (Edinburgh, 1794), Vol. 2, pp. 392–3. See also Heimann and McGuire, 'Newtonian forces and Lockean powers', pp. 281–93.

37 James Hutton, *Dissertations on Different Subjects in Natural Philosophy* (Edinburgh, 1792), pp. 290, 292.

38 Hutton, *Dissertations*, p. 669.

39 Hutton, *Investigation*, Vol. 2, p. 399; *idem*, *Dissertations*, p. 669.

40 Hutton, *Investigation*, Vol. 2, p. 407.

41 Hutton, *Dissertations*, p. 315.

42 Hutton, *Investigation*, Vol. 2, pp. 387, 404.

43 Hutton, *Investigation*, Vol. 2, p. 407; *idem*, *Dissertations*, pp. 297, 501; *idem*, *A Dissertation upon the Philosophy of Light, Heat and Fire*, (Edinburgh, 1794), p. 262.

44 On the dissemination of Priestley's ideas see Heimann, 'Faraday's theories of matter and electricity', pp. 243–53.

45 Faraday, *Electricity*, Vol. 2, pp. 290, 293.

46 John Playfair, 'Biographical account of James Hutton' [1805], *The Works of John Playfair*, 4 vols. (Edinburgh, 1822), Vol. 4, pp. 85–6. See also R. Olson, 'The reception of Boscovich's ideas in Scotland', *Isis*, 60 (1969), 91–103.

47 Faraday, *Electricity*, Vol. 2, p. 293.

CHAPTER VI

Helmholtz: the principle of the conservation of energy

The problem of the physical sciences is to reduce natural phenomena to unchangeable forces of attraction and repulsion whose intensity is dependent upon distance. The solution of this problem is at the same time the condition of the complete comprehensibility of nature. . . . The reduction of phenomena to simple forces [is] . . . the only possible reduction which the phenomena would allow . . . [and is] the necessary conceptual form for understanding nature.[1]

§1. Helmholtz's reductionist ontology

In his seminal essay *Über die Erhaltung der Kraft* (1847) Helmholtz provided the first systematic and mathematical formulation of the principle of the conservation of energy. A cardinal feature of the work is his attempt to demonstrate that an ontology of matter and the forces associated with material entities provided the explanatory framework for the principle of the conservation of energy. To justify his mechanistic ontology of particles and forces acting at a distance Helmholtz appealed to Kant's metaphysics of nature, seeking to demonstrate the conformity of nature to the laws of Newtonian physics. Helmholtz's formulation of the principle of the conservation of energy is therefore linked to his assumption that natural phenomena were reducible to central forces of attraction and repulsion.

Helmholtz's theory of the conservation of energy was not only important in providing a systematic and mathematical formulation of the principle of the conservation of energy, but in stressing the unifying role of the energy concept in relation to an ontology of matter in motion and the programme of mechanical explanation. By the middle of the nineteenth century the concept of energy was being employed to provide the science of physics with a new and unifying conceptual framework, which brought the phenomena of physics within the mechanical view of nature, embracing heat, light and electricity together with mechanics in a single conceptual structure. The establishment of the mechanical view of nature, which supposed that matter in motion was the basis for physical conceptualisation, as the programme of physical theory, and of the concept of energy and the law of the conservation of energy as principles unifying all physical phenomena, was the distinctive feature of the conceptual structure of nineteenth-century physics. In expressing the relation between mechanics, heat, light, electricity and magnetism by conceiving these phenomena in terms of different manifestations of energy, Helmholtz formulated the law of the conservation of energy as a mechanical theorem, emphasising the unifying role of the energy concept as an expression of the mechanical view of nature. By 1850 the doctrine that all forms of energy were forms of mechanical energy served to establish the energy principle as the kernel of the mechanical view of nature.

Helmholtz's 1847 memoir thus has a central role in the conceptual development of physics in the nineteenth century. An understanding of Helmholtz's argument requires analysis of the transformation in the science of physics in the first half of the nineteenth century and its bearing on Helmholtz's work, as well as an account of the emergence of the energy physics of the 1850s and 1860s and its relation to Helmholtz's energy theory and mechanistic physics. The conceptual kernel of Helmholtz's 1847 essay was his claim that the reducibility of natural phenomena to central forces of attraction and repulsion was basic to his formulation of the principle of the conservation of energy.

To establish his claim that the central force principle was the presupposition of the complete intelligibility of nature, and that the conformity of nature to Newtonian laws of central forces was the only possible explanatory system, Helmholtz appealed to Kant's metaphysics of nature. Helmholtz sought to establish the primacy of the central force concept by providing a metaphysical foundation for the concept of central forces so as to demonstrate its intelligibility as a scientific concept. The intelligibility and necessity of the ontology of the mechanical view of nature was given justificatory sanction by an appeal to metaphysical argument. The relationship between Helmholtz's philosophical argument and Kant's metaphysics of nature is therefore fundamental to the rationale of Helmholtz's attempt to establish the mechanical conception of nature, and therefore to his view of the status of his energy theory within the framework of empirical physics. Helmholtz's appeal to metaphysical argument in support of his ontology demonstrates the importance of metaphysical foundations and the problem of substance in his energy theory.

§2. The principle of the conservation of energy

In eighteenth-century natural philosophy the programme of the mathematisation of physical phenomena achieved its major successes in the study of mechanics, where hypotheses about atoms and the nature of forces were eschewed. By contrast, heat and electricity were generally explained by the supposition of imponderable fluids of heat and electricity, which were envisaged as composed of mutually-repelling particles which were attracted to the particles of ordinary matter. The phenomena of electricity, heat and chemistry, which were explained in terms of interparticulate forces and ethereal fluids, stood apart from the quantitative science of mechanics, though by the late eighteenth century attempts were made to subject electricity and heat to mathematical analysis, a development which initiated the conceptual unification of the science of physics, bridging the disjunction between the speculative and generally qualitative physics of heat and electricity and the quantitative science of mechanics. The formulation of the law of the conservation of energy, which subsumed the phenomena of heat and electricity within the framework of mechanical principles, was of central importance in the development of a unified science of physics by 1850.

The scope and conceptual principles of natural philosophy

were transformed in the period 1800–25, fostered by important developments in French physics. Laplace and Poisson formulated a new universal physics based on the hypothesis of molecular motions and forces, a 'physical mechanics' applicable to the science of mechanics as well as to the optical, thermal and electrical phenomena which had traditionally been explained in terms of interparticulate forces.[2] Even though the Laplacian theory of molecular forces was displaced by the work of Fresnel and Fourier in optics and the theory of heat, the Laplacian reductionist ontology probably shaped Helmholtz's theory of physical reality. Moreover, the Laplacian emphasis on the unification of physics, bridging the disjunction between mechanics and the phenomena of heat, light and electricity, had an enduring impact on the development of physics in the nineteenth century.[3]

Fresnel's wave theory of light which supposed that light was propagated by the vibrations of a universal ether, brought optics within the framework of the mechanical view of nature. Fresnel envisaged a unified physics based on the mechanical properties of the ether; and by the 1830s the wave theory of light was generally accepted, and physicists sought to elaborate a coherent mechanical theory of optics. The mechanical theory of the optical ether established a paradigm for the programme of mechanical explanation. The publication of Fourier's *Analytical Theory of Heat* (1822) brought the study of heat within the framework of mathematical analysis previously only applied to mechanical problems, bridging the traditional conceptual dichotomy in physics. Fourier's work established a paradigm for a mathematical physics not confined to narrowly mechanical problems, a unified and quantitative physics. By the 1840s the ideal of a unified physics based on mathematisation and mechanical principles had become firmly established in the writings of physicists.[4]

The doctrine of the unity and interconversion of natural powers played an important role in the emergence of the unified physics of the nineteenth century, and was one of the strands that, transformed, became explicated as the principle of the conservation of energy by around 1850. The belief in the interconversion of natural powers or 'forces' and the unity of nature, grounded on an awareness of the relationships between the phenomena of heat, light, electricity and chemistry, was common in late eighteenth-century natural philosophy, frequently based on the unified ether theory, which emphasised the balance of 'forces', the unity and interconversion of natural phenomena, and the self-sufficiency of nature. While the theory of the unified ether and imponderable fluids was abandoned in the early nineteenth century, the concept of the unity and interconversion of natural phenomena had a continued and significant influence on the development of natural philosophy.

These ideas were especially important in the 1830s. The discovery of electromagnetism by Oersted and of electromagnetic induction by Faraday were important in establishing the implication of the interconversion of natural phenomena, the equivalence of natural powers. Divorced from the unified ether theory and reinforced by the new experimental discoveries of conversion processes, in the 1830s the doctrine of the unity and equivalence of natural powers or 'forces' was part of the fabric of physical theory.[5] The concept of the conversion of 'forces' was central to Faraday's physical world view, and he stated his belief in the fundamental unity of powers in his paper on the action of magnetism on light in 1845: 'the various forms under which the forces of matter are made manifest have one common origin; or in other words are so directly related and mutually dependent that they are convertible, as it were, one into another, and possess equivalents of power in their action'.[6] The conversion of natural powers implied their quantitative equivalence.

The assertion of the conversion and equivalence of heat and mechanical 'work' was central to the establishment of the principle of the conservation of energy. While eighteenth-century natural philosophers had formulated a concept of the conservation of mechanical energy, in the form of the Leibnizian conservation of living force, they had considered energy losses within mechanical systems to be isolated from nonmechanical processes. Recognising that there would be apparent losses of living force in the collision of inelastic bodies, Johann Bernoulli had suggested that the living force apparently lost is in fact consumed in deforming the bodies. Drawing on his theory that an elastic body could be represented by means of elastic springs, he argued that inelastic bodies were analogous to springs that were impeded from expanding after being compressed, so that 'some part of the living force, which appears to perish, is consumed in the compression of the bodies'.[7] Thus, while living force would be consumed in the compression of bodies, the living force would not be destroyed. By contrast, in discussing the apparent loss of living force in inelastic collision, Helmholtz argued that while living force was indeed consumed in the deformation of inelastic bodies, some living force was also consumed in the generation of heat.[8] The principle of energy conservation asserted the essential unity of thermal and mechanical processes, maintaining that apparent losses of energy in mechanical processes were to be explained by the generation of heat.

By the early nineteenth century the measure of 'living force' by mechanical 'work', the product of force times distance, was becoming familiar in treatises on mechanics, providing a measure of mechanical energy, and establishing a quantitative basis for the conceptualisation of conversion processes. By the early 1840s the quantitative equivalence of mechanical work and heat was emphasised by several physicists, notably Joule, whose early papers on the calculation of the conversion coefficient of heat and work, the 'mechanical value' or mechanical equivalent of heat, were known to Helmholtz. The assertion of the equivalence of heat and work brought mechanical processes explicitly into the network of conversion processes. Joule's demonstration in 1843 that mechanical work could be directly transformed into heat by friction, and his conclusion that 'wherever mechanical force [work] is expended, an exact equivalent of heat is *always* obtained', provided a quantitative measure of conversion processes and a demonstration of the essential unity of thermal and mechanical phenomena.[9] Nevertheless, unlike Helmholtz, Joule did not claim the formulation of a general principle of the conservation of energy, but had sought to demonstrate the mutual convertibility of heat and mechanical work.[10]

The law of the conservation of energy provided a conceptualisation of the interconversion of natural powers and a quantitative measure of conserved physical quantities.[11] Helmholtz's essay on the conservation of energy was thus a major contribution to natural philosophy, though its origins lie in his interest in physiology and his concern with the problem of animal heat. Together with some other German physiologists, Helmholtz sought to base physiology on physical principles, advocating a reductionist programme of physiological explanation.[12] The mechanistic ontology and philosophical argument of Helmholtz's paper provided a basis for this programme of physiological reductionism. In seeking to demonstrate that the body heat and muscular action produced by animals could be derived from the oxidation of foodstuffs, Helmholtz was influenced by Liebig's *Animal Chemistry* (1842). 'Liebig's attempt to derive physiological phenomena from known physical and chemical laws', as Helmholtz declared in a paper published in 1845, formed the basis of Liebig's theory that respiration was the only source of animal heat. Helmholtz accepted the chemical theory of animal heat, but emphasised that the intelligibility of Liebig's argument, that the chemical 'force' supplied from the oxidation of foodstuffs was the source of aimal heat, was dependent on the validity of the 'principle of the constancy of the force equivalents by the excitation of one force by another'. Helmholtz observed however that Liebig's principle of the indestructibility and transformability of natural powers or 'forces' was 'hitherto neither completely decided or acknowledged nor empirically supported'.

The crucial problem was the subsumption of the 'forces' which regulated the physiology of organisms under the framework of the physical and chemical laws operative in the organic realm. In Helmholtz's view this would be the case if the operations of all natural agents were subject to the law of the 'constancy of force'. He did not reject Liebig's use of special 'vital forces', interpreting Liebig's theory as supposing that organic life was the result of 'forces' which were modifications of those operative in the inorganic world and hence subject to the law of the constancy of force. The crucial issue was 'whether organic life is the effect of a self-perpetuating, unique force, or the result of forces operating also in inorganic nature but modified by the particular manner of their continual operation'. Helmholtz rejected the intelligibility of any such self-perpetuating force which was not subject to the principle of the 'constancy of force'.[13]

The denial of perpetual motion was fundamental to Helmholtz's commitment to the principle of the constancy of force. He stated his intention in *Über die Erhaltung der Kraft* as being to apply the principle that 'it is impossible by any combination of natural bodies to produce force continually from nothing' to all parts of physics.[14] In this essay he sought to demonstrate the principle of *Erhaltung der Kraft* ['conservation of force'] by a mathematical investigation of the conserved physical quantities. The concept of the 'conservation' or 'constancy of force' (as he originally termed it)[15] acquired a sense additional to denoting the indestructibility and transformability of natural powers, that of the conservation of energy. Helmholtz's usage of the expression *Erhaltung der Kraft* embraced the doctrine of the conversion of 'forces' (as employed by Faraday, Joule and Liebig) together with the law of the conservation of energy, which provided a quantitative measure of the conserved physical quantities.

§3. Energy physics

The term 'energy' was first used as a general and fundamental physical concept by William Thomson (later Lord Kelvin) in 1849. Thomson affirmed that 'nothing can be lost in the operations of nature—no energy can be destroyed',[16] stressing the implications of Joule's demonstration of the equivalence of heat and mechanical work. Thomson later declared that Joule's discovery of the conversion of heat into work had 'led to the greatest reform that physical science had experienced since the days of Newton', the development of the law of the conservation of energy. By the early 1850s Thomson was seeking to establish the science of physics on the energy concept, and his generalised used of the concept of energy, its unifying role linking all physical phenomena within a network of energy transformations, expressed the primacy of energy in physical science. He argued that energy could be divided into two classes which he termed 'statical' and 'dynamical'. Weights at a height, an electrified body, and a quantity of fuel, all contained stores of statical energy. Masses of matter in motion, the thermal motion of the particles of bodies, and a volume of space containing undulations of light, contained stores of dynamical energy. All forms of energy were conceived as forms of 'mechanical energy', and all the phenomena of nature were subsumed within a theory of mechanical explanation based on the energy concept.[17]

Thomson's energy physics was further developed by Rankine in a paper 'On general law of the transformation of energy' (1853). Stressing the fundamental status of the energy concept as a primary agent in nature, Rankine defined the framework of the science of physics in terms of the universal energy concept and the law of the conservation of energy. He declared that:

> the term *energy* is used to comprehend every affection of substances which constitutes or is commensurable with a power of producing change in opposition to resistance, and includes ordinary motion and mechanical power [work], chemical action, heat, light, electricity, magnetism, and all other powers, known or unknown, which are convertible or commensurable with these.[18]

Rankine replaced Thomson's classification of energy as statical or dynamical by the terms 'potential' and 'actual' energy, drawing on the philosophical distinction between potential and actual existence,[19] these terms being ultimately replaced by the (modern) terms 'potential' and 'kinetic' energy in Thomson and Tait's *Treatise on Natural Philosophy* (1867). Rankine stated the 'law of the conservation of energy', that 'the sum of the actual [kinetic] and potential energies in the universe is unchangeable'.[20]

On reviewing Rankine's paper Helmholtz pointed out that his own terms 'living force' [*lebendige Kraft*] and 'tensional force' [*Spannkraft*] were synonymous with the terms 'actual [kinetic]' and 'potential energy' introduced by Rankine.[21] In a lecture (written in English) on the 'Law of the conservation of force' (1861) Helmholtz noted with approval Rankine's introduction of the expression 'conservation of energy'. Helmholtz suggested that this should be the preferred usage rather than his own expression the 'conservation of force', because the law in question 'does not mean that the intensity of the natural forces is constant; but it relates more to the whole amount of power which can be gained by any natural process, and by which a certain amount of work can be done'.

The term 'energy' thus gave a more precise description of the conserved quantities, emphasising the distinction between conserved physical quantities (denoted by the concept of energy) and the concept of force as defined by Newton's laws of motion. Nevertheless it remained appropriate to use the term 'force' to denote a natural power or natural agent, and to use the expression the 'law of the conservation of force' to denote the indestructibility and transformability of natural 'agents' or 'physical forces'.[22] The physiological context of Helmholtz's work and his relation to Liebig clarifies his conceptual framework and terminology. Helmholtz thus indicated that his principle of *Erhaltung der Kraft* denoted both the indestructibility of natural powers and the law of the conservation of energy.

The distinction between concepts of force and energy is basic to Helmholtz's mathematical argument. He derives a general form of the principle of the conservation of living force, arguing that for the motion of a body acted on by a central force emanating from a fixed centre of force, the change of 'living force' was equal to the change in the 'tensional force', a quantity measured by the product of the intensity of the force and the distance between the body and the force centre. For the motion of a body under a system of central forces the increase of living force was equal to the sum of the tensional forces which correspond to the alteration of its distance. Helmholtz concludes that 'the sum of the tensional and living forces is always constant'; this is the 'principle of the conservation of force [*Erhaltung der Kraft*]'. Helmholtz's terms 'living force' and 'tensional force' correspond to 'kinetic energy' and 'potential energy', and the principle of *Erhaltung der Kraft* thus provides a mathematical statement of the law of the conservation of energy.

The derivation of the law of the conservation of energy is based on the assumption that the actions of bodies are determined by central forces of attraction and repulsion. Helmholtz argues that 'whenever natural bodies act upon each other by forces of attraction or repulsion, which are independent of time and velocity, the sum of their living forces and tensional forces must be constant; the maximum quantity of mechanical work which can be obtained from them is therefore fixed, finite.' He emphasises that if bodies did not act by central forces which were independent of time and velocity, and only a function of distance, the principle of *Erhaltung der Kraft* would not be valid.[23] The central force principle is therefore a necessary condition for the validity of the law of the conservation of energy.

Helmholtz thus states the law of the conservation of energy as a mechanical theorem, as a natural law which is grounded on his mechanistic ontology of particles and central forces of attraction and repulsion. Moreover, the ontology of the mechanical view of nature is given justificatory sanction by appeal to metaphysical foundations. Given the fundamental importance of the central force principle in Helmholtz's demonstration of the law of the conservation of energy, the analysis of his metaphysical argument is crucial to an understanding of his intentions.

§4. Helmholtz's metaphysical argument

In the 'Introduction' to *Über die Erhaltung der Kraft* Helmholtz declares that the reduction of phenomena to central forces was significant for the 'central and ultimate aim of physical science'. Helmholtz's motive for asserting the importance of philosophical foundations was a consequence of his claim that the explanation of phenomena by central forces was the 'condition of the complete comprehensibility of nature', and would thus yield knowledge of 'the ultimate invariable causes of natural processes'. The justification of these claims by the explication of metaphysical foundations was intended to establish the physical actuality of the central force laws.[24]

Helmholtz distinguishes between the discovery of 'general rules' (such as Boyle's law of gases) which were merely 'generic concepts' by which phenomena could be subsumed under experimental laws, conceived as empirical generalisations from observational data, and the elaboration of a theoretical physics which aims to ascertain the unknown causes of natural phenomena by comprehending them under the 'law of causality', and thus to discover the ultimate causes of phenomena acting 'according to an invariable law'. Helmholtz argues that the possibility of formulating a theoretical science rests on the assumption that nature is intelligible: the 'presupposition of its comprehensibility' was a necessary condition for the articula-

tion of physical laws. The law of causality is a presupposition of
the intelligibility of nature, and the discovery of ultimate and
invariable causes presupposes that nature is causally and
systematically structured.[25]

Helmholtz thus claims that the possibility of scientific
explanation requires nature to be considered as structured in
accordance with causal laws; but from this he moves to the
quite separate and more specialised claim that nature is in fact
regulated by Newtonian laws involving central forces. He seeks
to demonstrate that the discovery of the invariable causes by
which nature can be rendered intelligible requires the reduction of phenomena to central forces of attraction and
repulsion; this becomes the condition of the 'complete comprehensibility' of nature. The argument by which he attempts to
prove this claim involves four separate contentions.

1   The existence of matter corresponds to our awareness of a
passive, unchanging reality which is characterised by spatial
extension and 'quantity (mass)'. Matter in itself, viewed as
such a passive entity, can only be subject to one change, a
spatial change, *viz.* motion.

2   The analysis of the concept of matter furthermore requires
consideration of the 'qualitative differences' apparent in natural
phenomena. These differences cannot be explained in terms of
the motion of a merely passive entity; the explanation of the
qualitative differences of matter requires analysis of its 'capacity
to produce effects'. He argues that this can only be ascribed to
the action of forces. Helmholtz contends that in considering
matter as an entity capable of producing effects the concepts of
materiality and force are inseparable. The concept of 'pure
matter' would not have the capacity to produce effects, and a
'pure force' cannot be regarded as having an existence separate
from matter. The concepts of matter and force are both 'abstractions from reality', and he rejects the construal of matter as an
entity which produces effects, with the concept of force being an
'empty concept'. The concept of matter cannot but be considered in relation to the capacity of natural entities to produce
effects, and this necessarily requires consideration of forces: 'we
can perceive matter only through its forces, not in and of itself'.

3   Having demonstrated that physics is concerned with matter
and force, Helmholtz restates his claim that natural phenomena

should be reduced to unchangeable ultimate causes. The ultimate causes determining natural phenomena are forces, and hence natural phenomena must be referred back to ultimate causes which are to be sought in entities possessing 'unchangeable forces (ineradicable qualities)', as found in chemical elements. The universe is therefore to be considered as consisting of chemical elements possessing unchangeable qualities. Since the only possible changes in such a system are spatial changes, the forces involved are moving forces whose action is determined by their spatial relations. Natural phenomena are thus to be reduced to the motions of matter endowed with unchangeable forces.

4   Helmholtz goes on to consider our experience of bodies, arguing that when bodies are considered with respect to our experience of them it is apparent that motion is a change of spatial relations and can therefore only take place among extended bodies. Thus motion can only be experienced as a change in the spatial relations of at least two bodies relative to one another. Furthermore, force, which is the cause of such changes, can only be conceived in terms of the relations between at least two bodies and is therefore to be defined as the tendency of two bodies to change their relative positions. Since the spatial relations of bodies as considered in the science of mechanics are conceived in terms of mass points, and since the spatial relations of two points have reference solely to their distance apart, the force which two mass points exert on one another must be such as to cause an alteration in the distance between them. Hence the force is a force of attraction or repulsion whose intensity is dependent solely on the distance between mass points.[26]

Helmholtz concludes that the aim of physics was the reduction of natural phenomena to 'unchangeable forces of attraction and repulsion whose intensity is dependent upon distance', contending that this would provide the condition for the 'complete comprehensibility of nature'. Moreover, it was the 'necessary conceptual form for understanding nature' and was 'the only possible one which the phenomena would allow'.[27] Helmholtz's appeal to philosophical argument in justification of his reductionist ontology was an acknowledgement that these claims could not be established empirically but demanded independent justification.

§5. Helmholtz and Kant

On editing *Über die Erhaltung der Kraft* for publication in the first volume of his collected papers in 1881, Helmholtz appended a note intended to clarify and reassess the philosophical argument of the 'Introduction' to the essay. Helmholtz points out that the philosophical argument had been 'more strongly influenced by Kant's epistemological insights than I would now consider still as correct'. He adds that 'only later' had he come to grasp that 'the principle of causality is in fact nothing but the presupposition of the lawlikeness of all natural phenomena'. The term 'cause' denotes the permanent reality beneath the change of appearance, *viz.* matter, whose law of action is manifested in forces. The concept of law requires that action be necessarily grounded in the action of matter and hence in the agency of force, and Helmholtz concludes that force taken in abstraction from matter would be tantamount to an hypostatisation of law, lacking the required conditions for exercising causal efficacy.[28]

Helmholtz clearly thought that this argument, from the universal lawlikeness of nature to its expression in terms of the material action of forces, provided a stronger justificational foundation for the central forces principle. It is significant that in the 1881 note he states that the original argument had been 'more strongly' influenced by Kant's philosophy than he would now accept, not that he wishes to disavow all Kantian metaphysical foundations. His 1881 claim that the principle of causality is equivalent to the lawlikeness of natural phenomena is similar to his assertion in the 1847 'Introduction' that the law of causality is a presupposition of the intelligibility of nature, arguments that clearly resemble Kant's view of causality as an expression of the lawlikeness of nature. Moreover, Helmholtz's emphasis in the 1881 note on the conceptual connection between the nature of law, force and matter displays distinct affinities with some of Kant's remarks in the *Critique of Pure Reason*, that causality implies action and force and presupposes the permanence of substance.[29]

Helmholtz's approach in both periods is broadly Kantian in outline, and his repudiation of the Kantian argument of the 1847 'Introduction' may simply have been intended as a rejection of his more systematic appeal to the argument of Kant's *Metaphysical Foundations* in 1847. As will be shown below, his appeal to the framework of the *Metaphysical Foundations* in the 'Introduction' to his 1847 essay is fundamental to his demonstration of the intelligibility of the central forces principle.

It is clear that Helmholtz did appreciate that the construal of causality as a presupposition of the lawlikeness of nature (as he asserts in both 1847 and 1881) was a distinctly Kantian doctrine, for in the third volume of his *Treatise on Physiological Optics* (1867) he discussed causality and lawlikeness and explicitly acknowledged the Kantian influence on his arguments. Helmholtz claims, using characteristically Kantian phraseology, that the law of causality is a 'law of our thinking' which is 'prior to all experience'. The possibility of our comprehending nature presupposes that the law of causality is 'a characteristic function of the intellect' as a result of which it 'can conceive of the world only as being in causal connection'.[30] This is evidently an explication of a view of the law of causality which accords with Kant's conception of causality as a transcendental condition, that the principle of causality not only makes experience possible but experience itself comes to possess a lawlike character. In the *Critique of Pure Reason* Kant argues that the principle of causality establishes the necessary ground for the conformity of nature to law.[31]

In the *Treatise on Physiological Optics* Helmholtz also argues that 'we have to proceed on the assumption that phenomena are comprehensible . . . that natural phenomena are to be subsumed under a definite causal connection', because if 'we cannot trace natural phenomena to a law, and therefore cannot make the law objectively effective as being the cause of the phenomena, the very possibility of comprehending such phenomena ceases'.[32] It is this sense of causality which Kant suggests in arguing that lawlikeness is a presupposition of the comprehensibility of empirical laws, and hence that the possibility of the construction of the framework of theoretical science presupposes that nature be considered as causally structured.[33] This sense of causality is alluded to by Helmholtz in his 1847 'Introduction', in claiming that it was a 'presupposition of its comprehensibility' that nature could be rendered intelligible only in terms of invariable causal laws, and again in his 1881 note where he claims that the law of causality was the 'presupposition of the lawlikeness of all natural phenomena'.[34]

It seems most unlikely that Helmholtz ever distinguished clearly between causality as a transcendental condition and causality as a condition of the possibility of empirical laws as members of systematic theories. Both senses of lawlikeness appear in his treatment of the causal principle in the *Treatise on Physiological Optics*, and the concept of causality as a presupposition of the comprehensibility of laws does correspond to Helmholtz's 1847 claim that the law of causality was a necessary condition for the intelligibility of nature. The ease with which Helmholtz could slide from the concept of lawlikeness as a transcendental condition to the concept of lawlikeness as a condition for the intelligibility of nature in the *Treatise* suggests that the argument in the 1847 'Introduction' embodied a similar but implicit conflation.

The distinctive feature of the 1847 'Introduction' is Helmholtz's attempt to demonstrate that the discovery of the invariable causes by which nature can be rendered intelligible requires the reduction of the phenomena to central forces. It is this argument that he rejects in 1881, acknowledging his earlier indebtedness to Kantian metaphysics. Helmholtz's demonstration of the intelligibility of the central force principle is suggestive of Kant's fourfold metaphysical explication of the concept of matter in the *Metaphysical Foundations*. Helmholtz's intention in the 'Introduction', to demonstrate that the intelligibility of nature requires the reduction of phenomena to Newtonian laws of central forces, has affinities to Kant's intention in the *Metaphysical Foundations*, to demonstrate the possibility of Newtonian physics. While Kant was concerned to establish a system of mathematical physics based on concepts whose possibility was established by the elaboration of metaphysical principles, Helmholtz sought to establish the claim that the invariable laws which render nature intelligible were Newtonian laws, appealing to metaphysical argument in his attempt to explicate an ontology of matter and central forces.

The parallels between Helmholtz's argument and Kant's metaphysical explication of the concept of matter can be seen by a comparison of the structure of Helmholtz's argument and the framework of Kant's *Metaphysical Foundations*.

1   Kant's concern with matter as an extensive magnitude in the chapter on 'Phoronomy', corresponding to the category of quantity, so that matter is viewed solely in terms of its motion, has analogies with Helmholtz's discussion of matter as a passive entity which is characterised by the concept of quantity and can only be subject to one change, that of motion.

2   Kant's argument in the chapter on 'Dynamics' that the qualitative differences of matter are to be explained by means of its forces, bears some analogies to Helmholtz's claim that the qualitative differences in natural phenomena are to be explained in terms of the capacity which matter possesses for the production of effects, and that this can only be ascribed to the action of forces. Helmholtz therefore emphasises the inseparability of matter and force.

3   Kant's argument in the chapter on 'Mechanics' that the relations of material entities are to be explicated in terms of the motion of the moving forces of matter, in terms of spatial changes, corresponds to Helmholtz's assertion that natural phenomena are to be explained in terms of moving forces whose action is determined by their spatial relations, and hence that phenomena are to be reduced to the motions of matter endowed with unchangeable moving forces.

4   Kant's discussion in the chapter on 'Phenomenology' of the relation of matter to our experience of it, in terms of its motion, its forces and the relation between the moving forces, corresponds to Helmholtz's argument that matter is experienced through its motion, its forces, and the action between bodies and their forces.[35]

There are therefore clear structural analogies between the argument of the *Metaphysical Foundations* and Helmholtz's attempt to provide justificatory sanction for the intelligibility of his central forces principle. Although Helmholtz did not construct his argument with explicit reference to the Kantian metaphysical explication of the concept of matter, these textual affinities and his own later admission of the Kantian influence strongly suggest that he had Kant's metaphysics in mind.[36] There is however no hint in Helmholtz's discussion of Kant's reappraisal of the metaphysical assumptions of Newton's theory of nature, notably Kant's account of his 'metaphysico-dynamical' concept of matter which claimed that the concept of matter was to be explicated in terms of fundamental forces of attraction and repulsion which defined its physical basis. By contrast, Helmholtz contends that the concepts of matter and force are both abstractions from reality, and that both these concepts are required in characterising the capacity of natural entities to produce effects. Hence physical phenomena are to be explained in terms of the concepts of matter and force.

There are moreover important differences in intention between Kant's demonstration of the possibility of Newtonian science and Helmholtz's demonstration that the reduction of phenomena to Newtonian laws of central forces would render nature intelligible. These differences are of fundamental importance in delineating Helmholtz's own objectives. Kant's purpose was to demonstrate the possibility of Newtonian physics, the law of gravity and the laws of motion, by appeal to metaphysical foundations, not to claim that the actual inductive validity of Newtonian physics was meant to follow from the transcendental principles. The demonstration of the links between the categories and physical concepts and laws was meant to establish the possibility of Newtonian physics, not its physical actuality. By contrast, Helmholtz clearly believed that his account of the metaphysics of corporeal nature would demonstrate the actual conformity of nature to Newtonian laws. In Helmholtz's view the Newtonian laws of central forces were 'the necessary conceptual form for understanding nature . . . the only possible one which the phenomena would allow',[37] and his appeal to Kantian metaphysics was an attempt at justification of these claims.

Helmholtz construed his metaphysical argument as having the strength of a quasi-deductive demonstration, a consequence of the insufficient recognition of the Kantian distinction between actuality and possibility. His fundamental assumption was that the reduction of phenomena to central forces was the condition of the complete intelligibility of nature, and by relating his physical arguments closely to metaphysical principles he sought to justify this claim and in consequence the physical actuality of the central force laws themselves.

§6. Helmholtz and mechanical explanation

In an essay of 1877 on Helmholtz's contributions to science, Maxwell declared that the great merit of Helmholtz's formulation of the law of the conservation of energy was his demonstration that the principle of energy conservation determined the configuration and motion of the particles constituting bodies, even when the particles could not be observed. The law of energy conservation was a mechanical theorem, based on Helmholtz's demonstration that it was grounded on a mechanistic ontology of particles and forces acting at a distance.[38]

Maxwell thus located the unique importance of Helmholtz's 1847 essay in its relation to the programme of mechanical explanation which exerted a dominating influence on the development of physics in the ninteenth century. Thomson and Tait's *Treatise on Natural Philosophy* (1867) had an important impact on these developments, incorporating the law of the conservation of energy into the framework of analytical dynamics. Thomson and Tait argued that the energy of a material system, determined by the configuration and motion of the parts of the system, could be specified without reference to the hidden mechanism determining the configuration and motion of the system.[39] The universal significance of the law of the conservation of energy was therefore a consequence of its role in subsuming the motions of the unobservable particles of a material system within the framework of mechanical explanation, without the need for the formulation of hypotheses about the hidden mechanical structure of the system.[40]

Helmholtz's adherence to a reductionist ontology of matter and central forces was basic to his commitment to the intelligibility of the mechanical view of nature. He refused to envisage any deviation from the fundamental principles that he had first expounded in 1847. His refusal to countenance any relaxation of the applicability of these principles is apparent in the controversy over the theory of electricity in the 1870s, which challenged Helmholtz's continued espousal of the central force principle. Physicists speculated that the law of the conservation of energy required modification in its application to the theory of electricity, and that Newton's law of action and reaction need not hold for electrical forces, while others suggested that electric action was propagated with a finite velocity. By contrast, Helmholtz sought to derive a formalism that did not introduce a time-dependent force law and hence was consistent with his energy physics.[41] In his 1881 notes to his essay on the conservation of energy Helmholtz emphasised that any abrogation of the central force principle by denying 'the established mechanical principles of the equality of action and reaction and of the constancy of energy' would be an abandonment of any prospect of 'the complete solution of scientific problems'.[42] The acceptance of such theories threatened a violation of the principles which were a necessary condition of the intelligibility of nature.

In *Über die Erhaltung der Kraft* Helmholtz had attempted to establish the central force principle by an appeal to metaphysical foundations. In grounding the law of the conservation of energy on a reductionist ontology of particles and central forces Helmholtz did not only establish its status as a mechanical theorem, but also as a universal principle of physics. All physical phenomena were subsumed under the law of energy conservation, enunciated as a mechanical theorem and grounded on a mechanistic ontology. For Helmholtz, his claim of the complete intelligibility of nature in virtue of the reducibility of phenomena to central forces was grounded on his appeal to metaphysical foundations; hence the principle of the conservation of energy was formulated explicitly in terms of a mechanistic ontology, a world view which he believed to have received a metaphysical sanction and thus possessed a special status.

Notes

1 Hermann von Helmholtz, *Über die Erhaltung der Kraft* [1847], *Wissenschaftliche Abhandlungen*, 3 vols. (Leipzig, 1882–95), Vol. 1, pp. 16–17. Translated as 'On the conservation of force', in *Scientific Memoirs, Natural Philosophy*, ed. J. Tyndall and W. Francis (London, 1853), pp. 114–62. There is a revision of this translation in R. Kahl, ed., *Selected Writings of Hermann von Helmholtz* (Middletown, Conn., 1971), pp. 3–55. I have consulted both these translations, but frequently differ from them.

2 S. D. Poisson, 'Mémoire sur l'équilibre et le mouvement des corps

élastiques', *Mém. Acad. Sci.*, 8 (1829), 361. *Cf.* R. Fox, 'The rise and fall of Laplacian physics', *Hist. Stud. Phys. Sc.*, 3 (1974), 89–136.

3 P. M. Harman, *Energy, Force, and Matter. The Conceptual Development of Nineteenth-Century Physics* (Cambridge, 1982), pp. 12–19.

4 Harman, *Energy, Force, and Matter*, pp. 21–30.

5 Harman, *Energy, Force, and Matter*, pp. 30–5.

6 M. Faraday, *Experimental Researches in Electricity*, 3 vols. (London, 1839–55), Vol. 3, p. 1.

7 J. Bernoulli, 'De vera notione virium vivarum' [1735], *Opera Omnia*, 4 vols. (Lausanne, 1742), pp. 242–3. *Cf.* P. M. Heimann, '"Geometry and nature"', *Centaurus*, 21 (1977), 15–16, and E. Hiebert, *Historical Roots of the Principle of the Conservation of Energy* (Madison, 1962), pp. 87–94.

8 Helmholtz, *Abhandlungen*, Vol. 1, pp. 31–2.

9 J. P. Joule, 'The mechanical value of heat' [1843], *The Scientific Papers of James Prescott Joule*, 2 vols. (London, 1884–7), Vol. 1, pp. 123, 158.

10 See W. Thomson, 'On the dynamical theory of heat' [1851], *Mathematical and Physical Papers*, 6 vols. (Cambridge, 1882–1911), Vol. 1, p. 175.

11 Harman, *Energy, Force, and Matter*, pp. 35–41.

12 P. F. Cranefield, 'The organic physics of 1847 and the biophysics of today', *J. Hist. Med.*, 12 (1957), 407–23.

13 H. Helmholtz, 'Über den Stoffverbrauch bei der Muskelaction' [1845], *Abhandlungen*, Vol. 2, p. 735; *idem*, 'Theorie der physiologische Wärmeerscheinungen für 1845', *Abhandlungen*, Vol. 1, p. 6. On Liebig see T. O. Lipman, 'Vitalism and reductionism in Liebig's physiological thought', *Isis*, 58 (1967), 167–85.

14 Helmholtz, *Abhandlungen*, Vol. 1, p. 17.

15 Helmholtz used the phrase *Constanz der Kraft* in letters to du Bois-Reymond of 21 December 1846, 12 February 1847 and 21 July 1847: see P. M. Heimann, 'Helmholtz and Kant: the metaphysical foundations of *Über die Erhaltung der Kraft*', *Stud. Hist. Phil. Sci.*, 5 (1974), 207. Helmholtz also used this phrase in the published memoir, *Abhandlungen*. Vol. 1, p. 27.

16 William Thomson, 'An account of Carnot's theory of the motive power of heat' [1849], *Papers*, Vol. 1, p. 118 n. See Harman, *Energy, Force, and Matter*, pp. 60–4; and C. W. Smith, 'A new chart for British natural philosophy: the development of energy physics in the nineteenth century', *Hist. Sci.*, 16 (1978), 231–79.

17 W. Thomson, 'On the mechanical antecedents of motion, heat and light' [1854], *Papers*, Vol. 2, p. 34; *idem*, 'On a universal tendency in nature to the dissipation of mechanical energy' [1852], *Papers*, Vol. 1, p. 511.

18 W. J. M. Rankine, 'On the general law of the transformation of energy', *Phil. Mag.*, 5 (1853), 106.

19 *Cf.* William Hamilton, *Lectures on Metaphysics and Logic*, 4 vols., ed. H. L. Mansel and J. Veitch (Edinburgh, 1859), Vol. 1, pp. 179 f.

20 W. Thomson and P. G. Tait, *Treatise on Natural Philosophy* (Oxford, 1867), p. 195; Rankine, 'Law of the transformation of energy', p. 106.

21 H. Helmholtz, 'Theorie der Wärme', *Fortschritte der Physik in Jahre 1853* (Berlin, 1856), p. 407.

22 H. Helmholtz, 'On the application of the law of the conservation of force to organic nature' [1861], *Abhandlungen*, Vol. 3, pp. 565–6, 579.

23 Helmholtz, *Abhandlungen*, Vol. 1, pp. 25, 27.

24 Helmholtz, *Abhandlungen*, Vol. 1, pp. 12, 16, 13.

25 Helmholtz, *Abhandlungen*, Vol. 1, p. 13.

26 Helmholtz, *Abhandlungen*, Vol. 1, pp. 14–15.

27 Helmholtz, *Abhandlungen*, Vol. 1, pp. 16–17.

28 Helmholtz, *Abhandlungen*, Vol. 1, p. 68.

29 I. Kant, *Critique of Pure Reason*, B249/B250.

30 H. von Helmholtz, *Handbuch der physiologischen Optik*, 3 vols. (Leipzig, 1856–67), Vol. 3, pp. 453, 455.

31 Kant, *Critique*, B165. See above pp. 58–9.

32 Helmholtz, *Handbuch*, Vol. 3, p. 455.

33 See above p. 59.

34 Helmholtz, *Abhandlungen*, Vol. 1, pp. 13, 68.

35 *Cf.* above pp. 116–17.

36 For discussion of Helmholtz's interest in Kant and the Kantian intellectual environment in which he worked see: L. Koenigsberger, *Hermann von Helmholtz*, trans. F. A. Welby (Oxford, 1906), p. 18; Heimann, 'Helmholtz and Kant', pp. 209, 229–32; D. H. Galaty, 'The philosophical basis of mid-nineteenth-century German reductionism', *J. Hist. Med.*, 29 (1974), 295–316.

37 Helmholtz, *Abhandlungen*, Vol. 1, p. 17.

38 J. C. Maxwell, 'Helmholtz' [1877], *The Scientific Papers of James Clerk Maxwell*, ed. W. D. Niven, 2 vols (Cambridge, 1890), Vol 2, pp. 593–4.

39 *Cf.* D. F. Moyer, 'Energy, dynamics, hidden machinery: Rankine, Thomson and Tait, Maxwell', *Stud. Hist. Phil. Sci.*, 8 (1977), 251–68.

40 *Cf.* J. C. Maxwell, *Matter and Motion* (London, 1877), pp. 68–71; *idem*, 'Thomson and Tait's Natural Philosophy' [1879], *Papers*, Vol. 2, pp. 782–4.

41 Helmholtz, 'Über die Bewegungsgleichungen der Elektricität' [1870], *Abhandlungen*, Vol. 1, pp. 543–628. See M. N. Wise, 'German concepts of force, energy and the electromagnetic ether: 1845–1880', in *Conceptions of Ether*, ed. G. N. Cantor and M. J. S. Hodge (Cambridge, 1981), pp. 269–307, and Heimann, 'Helmholtz and Kant', pp. 235–7.

42 Helmholtz, *Abhandlungen*, Vol. 1, pp. 69–70.

CHAPTER VII

Maxwell: dynamical explanation and the problem of substance

What I propose now to do is to examine the consequences of the assumption that the phenomena of the electric current are those of a moving system, the motion being communicated from one part of the system to another by forces, the nature and laws of which we do not yet even attempt to define, because we can eliminate these forces from the equations of motion by the method given by Lagrange for any connected system.[1]

§1. Field theory and the dynamical world view

In his *Treatise on Electricity and Magnetism* (1873) Maxwell elaborated a theory of the electromagnetic field by employing a formalism which avoided the explication of the nature of the material substance constituting physical reality. Maxwell formulated a theory of mechanical explanation in which matter was conceived as a mathematical entity rather than as a substantial reality. The concept of inertia was not considered as an essential property of matter but as defined by its functional role in the abstract formalism of mechanical principles. Analysing the metaphysical assumptions of matter theory, Maxwell sought to distinguish between the concept of matter as the material substratum of bodies and a functional concept of matter as defined by the symbolism of mechanical principles. The structure of the hidden mechanism constituting the electromagnetic field was not represented, and the forces between the particles of the hidden mechanism were not considered in the analytical formalism of Maxwell's mechanical principles.

The relation between mathematical and physical representation was a major problem in Maxwell's natural philosophy.
He explored the role of physical analogies which could provide
a physical embodiment of mathematical equations without the
assumption of an insufficiently validated physical hypothesis.
While he discussed the applicability of a mechanical analogy as
a model of the hidden structure of the field, he questioned the
assumption that the unobservable structure of the mechanism
constituting the field could be represented by a mechanical
model whose properties were based on the properties of
observable particles of matter. Hence the mechanical structure
of the mechanism of the field was not formulated, in favour of
its representation by the Lagrangian formalism of mechanical
principles.

In seeking to justify his appeal to a theory of the physical field
grounded on the hidden mechanism of the ether, Maxwell
appealed to Newton's letter to Bentley, where Newton had
declared that it was inconceivable that matter could interact at
a distance without the action of a mediating agent. In support
of the concept of a mediating ether Maxwell declares that it was
'more philosophical to admit the existence of a medium . . .
than to assert that a body can act at a place where it is not'.
Maxwell quoted Colin Maclaurin's discussion of Newton's
ether concept in his *Account of Sir Isaac Newton's Philosophical
Discoveries* (1748), emphasising that Newton had developed a
theory of an ethereal medium to explain gravitational attraction. Maxwell was thus searching for a Newtonian pedigree for
his denial of action at a distance.[2]

Maxwell's field theory was a major contribution to physical
theory. In his paper 'A dynamical theory of the electromagnetic
field' (1865), Maxwell explained that 'the theory I propose may
therefore be called a theory of the *Electromagnetic Field*, because
it has to do with the space in the neighbourhood of the electric
or magnetic bodies, and it may be called a *Dynamical* Theory,
because it assumes that in that space there is matter in motion,
by which the observed electromagnetic phenomena are produced'. The concept of a field was to be contrasted with an
action-at-a-distance theory of electric action, a distinction
contrasting the mediating agency of the contiguous elements of
the 'field' existing in the space between separated electrified

bodies and central forces acting directly between electrified bodies across finite distances of space. In a field theory the forces between bodies were mediated by some property of the ambient space or field, and Maxwell formulated a 'dynamical' theory that assumed that electromagnetic phenomena were produced by the motions of particles of matter, that action was transmitted in the field by a 'complicated mechanism capable of a vast variety of motion'.

Maxwell's use of the term 'dynamics' must therefore be sharply differentiated from Leibnizian or Kantian usage: for Maxwell the mechanical or 'dynamical' world view, which supposed on ontology of particles of matter in motion as the substratum underlying physical reality, was fundamental to the programme of physics, the explanation of physical phenomena by the structure and laws of motion of a mechanical system. Maxwell emphasises that according to his 'dynamical theory of the electromagnetic field' the mechanism of the field was 'subject to the general laws of Dynamics'; in this conception of 'dynamical theory' the mechanism of the field was represented by the Lagrangian formalism of analytical dynamics rather than the explication of a specific mechanical model of its physical structure.[3]

Maxwell emphasises the gap between the presupposition of the ontology of the mechanical world view and the invention of hypothetical mechanical models of the field. He argues that it was impossible to elaborate a unique mechanical model of the field, and maintains that the equations of motion of the Lagrangian formalism of dynamics were independent of the structure of the connections of the mechanical system constituting the field. While Maxwell's interpretation of Lagrangian dynamical theory stresses the physical status of dynamical concepts, not merely their symbolic role in the generalised equations of motion (as in Lagrange's own exposition of the method of analytical dynamics), he emphasises that the intelligibility of concepts of force and inertia was grounded on the dynamical formalism and was detached from ontological foundations.

Newton too had declared that the meaning of the concept of force was defined by the mathematical formalism of *Principia*, but the intelligibility of Newton's concept of force is grounded on his disjunction between the concepts of force and inertia and on his explication of the nature of matter. Maxwell's discussion of the metaphysical foundations of Newtonian physics high-lighted the problematic status of matter theory in the conceptual foundations of Newton's theory of mechanics. In his analysis of metaphysical foundations Maxwell stresses the disjunction between material reality and the framework of dynamical theory. The rationale of his interpretation of the conceptual status of the formalism of dynamical principles is grounded on his metaphysical explication of the relation between substantial and functional representation.

§2. Mathematical and physical representation: physical analogy

The inclusive breadth of Maxwell's definition of the concept of the field embraces both of Faraday's formulations of field theory: a theory which supposed the primacy of lines of force in space, and a theory which postulated the mediation of action by means of the contiguous particles of a space-pervading substance, the dielectric medium. These alternative modes of representation of the field were each subjected to comprehensive mathematical and conceptual development by Maxwell. Maxwell explored the geometrical implications of Faraday's theory of physical lines of force, and he proposed a mechanical theory of the ether—by analogy with the mechanical theories of the optical ether which were firmly established in physics—to represent the transmission of action in the field by a mechanism of ether particles. Emphasising that the forces between bodies were mediated by some property of the ambient field, Maxwell developed Faraday's theories in an attempt to resolve the fundamental conceptual issue raised by Faraday: the relationship between the mode of propagation of force in the field and the nature of the material substance constituting the physical structure of the field.[4]

In his first theory of the field, 'On Faraday's lines of force' (1856), Maxwell elaborates a purely geometrical representation of the structure of the field based on Faraday's concept of lines of force. In this 'geometrical model' of the field the directions of the forces acting in the field were represented by lines of force filling space, the intensity of the forces being represented by an incompressible fluid moving in tubes formed by lines of force. He emphasises that the fluid was 'not even a hypothetical fluid' but 'merely a collection of imaginary properties'. The geometrical model of fluid flow was a 'physical analogy' which presented 'the mathematical ideas to the mind in an embodied form'.[5]

For Maxwell the relation between the mathematical and physical representation of phenomena was a problem of fundamental importance. From his letters to William Thomson (later Lord Kelvin) in 1854–5 it is apparent that Maxwell was interested in a paper of Thomson's on the geometrical analogy between thermal and electrical phenomena. Thomson had employed a mathematical formalism for electrostatics analogous to the mathematical theory of the distribution of heat elaborated by Fourier in his *Analytical Theory of Heat* (1822), proposing a geometrical model, common to both electrostatic attraction and thermal conduction, in which the distribution of electricity was represented by a flux of electrical force and the distribution of heat was represented by a flux of heat.[6] Thomson's 'allegorical representation' of electrostatics, as Maxwell describes it, provided the mathematical formalism appropriate to the geometrical representation of lines of force: 'I have been planning and partly executing a system of propositions about lines of force &c which may be *afterwards* applied to Electricity, Heat or Magnetism or Galvanism, but which is in itself a collection of purely geometrical truths embodied in geometrical conceptions of lines, surfaces &c'.[7]

Maxwell emphasises that although the concept of fluid flow was suggested by the mathematical analogy between the flow of heat and the flow of electrical force, this geometrical representation did not have the status of a physical hypothesis; it was rather a 'physical analogy' grounded on a 'resemblance in mathematical form between two different phenomena'. He underlines this point most emphatically in a draft of the paper: 'while the mathematical laws of the conduction of heat derived from the idea of heat as a substance are admitted to be true, the theory of heat has been so modified that we can no longer apply to it the idea of substance'.[8] The notions of mathematical resemblance and physical analogy expressed Maxwell's desire to avoid the dangers of a premature physical theory while at the same time expressing the mathematical ideas in a form 'more applicable to physical problems than that in which algebraic symbols alone are used'. Hence the representation of lines of force by the flow of an incompressible fluid provided a physical embodiment of mathematical theorems, its introduction sanctioned by the appeal to mathematical resemblance and physical analogy.[9]

Maxwell thus seeks to chart the relation between mathematical and physical representation by an appeal to analogical argument. In an essay on 'Analogies in nature' written in 1856 he developed his concept of the role of analogies by arguing that 'although pairs of things may differ widely from each other, the *relation* in the one pair may be the same as that in the other . . . as in a scientific point of view the *relation* is the most important thing to know, a knowledge of the one thing leads us a long way towards a knowledge of the other'. In arguing that the object of knowledge is relation, Maxwell's construal of the role of analogical argument echoes the views of Scottish philosophers, imbibed from his professor of philosophy at Edinburgh, William Hamilton, that knowledge involves the comparison of experiences.[10] As he later observed, the mathematical analogy between fluid flow, the distribution of heat and electrostatic attraction implied mathematical resemblance not physical similarity, for 'the similarity is a similarity between relations, not a similarity between the things related'.[11] The role of physical analogies was therefore the explication of mathematical relations presented in an embodied form, to avoid the 'rashness in assumption' of a physical theory insufficiently validated by experiment while at the same time anchoring the symbolic representation to a physical analogy so as not to 'lose sight of the phenomena to be explained'.[12]

In consonance with his distinction between a mathematical formalism and a physical hypothesis Maxwell presents his interpretation of Faraday's theory of lines of force as a geometrical representation of the spatial distribution of force in the field rather than as a physical model of the constitution of the field. In a draft of the paper he observes that 'Faraday treats the distribution of forces in space as the primary phenomenon, and does not insist on any theory as to the nature of the centres of force round which these forces are generally but not always grouped'. In the published paper he affirms that Faraday's concept of lines of force provided 'a geometrical model of the physical phenomena'; he did not accept Faraday's physical interpretation of lines of force which depicted the field as a plenum of force, a theory of the field which was grounded on Faraday's concept of matter defined in terms of its inherent forces diffused through space.[13]

In the *Treatise* Maxwell remarked that Faraday 'even speaks of the lines of force belonging to a body as in some sense part of itself, so that in its action on distant bodies it cannot be said to act where it is not'. Maxwell declared that this notion was 'not a dominant idea with Faraday', denying that this theory of matter should be construed as an essential presupposition of Faraday's theory of a 'field of force'. Maxwell thus interprets Faraday's concept of the field as supposing that 'the field of space is full of lines of force, whose arrangement depends on that of the bodies in the field'. The theory of lines of force represented the spatial distribution, the disposition, direction and intensity of the forces, and did not imply that the physcial constitution of the field was to be envisaged as a plenum of force which defined the essence of material substances.[14]

The essentially geometrical focus of Maxwell's theory of lines of force is emphasised in a letter he wrote to Faraday in 1857, in which he discusses the possibility of elaborating the concept of lines of force to explain gravitation. 'The lines of Force from the Sun spread out from him and when they come near a planet *curve out from it* so that every planet diverts a number depending on its mass from their course and substitutes a system of its own so as to become something like a comet, *if lines of force were visible*'.[15]

It was the geometrical imagery of lines of force that excited Maxwell's interest. Nevertheless he envisaged the possibility of formulating a physical theory of the field. In his paper 'On Faraday's lines of force' he announced his intention to elaborate a 'mechanical conception' of Faraday's theory of the electrotonic state, a concept which Faraday had employed to represent the field envisaged as a state of tension of the particles of the ambient dielectric medium (and which Faraday had abandoned in favour of the theory of physical lines of force). Maxwell indicated that he envisaged the physical representation of the electro-tonic state by means of a study of the theory of the ether, referring to a paper published in 1847 in which William Thomson had considered the propagation of electric and magnetic forces in terms of the linear and rotational strain of an elastic solid medium.[16] Maxwell thus sought a physical theory of the field in terms of the formulation of a theory of the ambient ether as the material substratum of the field. By the time Maxwell wrote to Faraday in 1857 he had learnt of an important paper of Thomson's published in the previous year, where Thomson had argued that the phenomenon of magneto-optic rotation discovered by Faraday could be explained by a vortical motion in the ether. Maxwell drew Faraday's attention to Thomson's work, remarking that this theory appeared to provide a basis for the 'confirmation of the physical nature of magnetic lines of force'.[17]

§3. Mechanical models and physical reality

Maxwell's intentions, foreshadowed in these remarks, were made explicit in the title of his paper 'On physical lines of force' (1861–2). In this paper he advances from a discussion of the physical geometry of lines of force to a treatment of the electromagnetic field 'from a mechanical point of view'. Maxwell develops a systematic physical model of the propagation of electrical and magnetic forces in terms of a stress in a 'magneto-electric medium'. He supposes that the magnetic field could be characterised as a fluid filled with rotating vortex tubes, their geometrical arrangement corresponding to the lines of force, and the angular velocities of the vortices corresponding to the intensity of the field. The vortex model is employed as a physical representation of the lines of force; abandoning the geometrical imagery of lines of force Maxwell now employs the concept of the electro-tonic state as a physical representation of the lines of force, providing a mechanical interpretation of the electro-tonic state as the rotational momentum of the vortices.

Maxwell suggested a mechanical analogy to explain the rotation of vortices about parallel axes in the same direction, drawing the analogy with a machine where an 'idle wheel' is placed between two wheels which were intended to revolve in the same direction. Supposing that a layer of particles, acting as idle wheels, were placed between contiguous vortices, he argues that these 'idle wheel' particles would be subjected to translational motion if adjacent vortices had different angular velocities, the motion of these particles corresponding to the flow of an electric current in an inhomogeneous magnetic field.[18]

Maxwell consistently emphasises that his model of idle wheel particles and an ether conceived as a cellular structure of vortices was merely a 'provisional and temporary' hypothesis. He confesses that the model might appear 'awkward', but notes that he did 'not bring it forward as a mode of connexion existing in nature'. The supposition of a 'mechanically conceivable' model of the ether merely demonstrated the possibility of a mechanical explanation of the field, a theory which explained the mediation of action in the field by the postulation of a mechanism of ether particles. In support of his contention that a mechanical explanation of the field was a necessary condition of its intelligibility Maxwell consistently appeals to Faraday's discovery of the rotatory effect of magnetism on light which, as he observes in the *Treatise*, indicated that 'some phenomenon of rotation is going on in the magnetic field' and which therefore required explication 'by means of some kind of mechanism', though the hypothesis of molecular vortices and idle wheel particles was merely suggestive and illustrative.[19]

Maxwell's theory of the field as a mechanism of ether particles brought the field concept into harmony with the mechanical theories of optics which had been firmly established in physics since the 1830s. The wave theory of light as undulations in a luminiferous ether, conceived as transverse vibrations at right angles to the direction of the propagated wave (like the undulations of a plucked cord) provided a paradigm for the explanation of the phenomena of physics by the construction of a mechanical model. The laws of optics and, by implication, those of other physical phenomena, could be brought within the framework of mechanical explanation, and rendered conceptually intelligible by reference to the mechanics of the ether, a programme of research which had shaped Thomson's attempt to explicate the propagation of electrical and magnetic forces in terms of the strain of an elastic solid ether.[20] While Maxwell's representation of the field by a mechanical ether model went beyond Thomson's purely mathematical treatment of the analogy between electromagnetism and the properties of an elastic solid ether, Maxwell insisted on the provisional character of his physical model. He succeeded in developing his ether model to achieve the unification of optics and electromagnetism, formulating a mechanical theory of the ether which had optical and electromagnetic correlates. He demonstrated that transverse elastic waves were transmitted in the ether with the same velocity as light waves, and concluded that 'we can scarcely avoid the inference that *light consists in the transverse undulations of the same medium which is the cause of electric and magnetic phenomena*'.[21]

Maxwell remained preoccupied with the epistemological status of his physical ether model. In a letter to P. G. Tait in 1867 he remarks that his ether model was 'built up to show that the phenomena can be explained by mechanism. The nature of the mechanism is to the true mechanism what an orrery is to the Solar System'.[22] The mechanical ether model was illustrative, like a working model of the planetary orbits, but also demonstrated the possibility of articulating a mechanical theory of the field. He returns to this theme in the *Treatise* emphasising that his earlier attempt 'to imagine a working model of this mechanism [of the ether] must be taken for no more than it really is, a demonstration that mechanism may be imagined capable of producing a connexion mechanically equivalent to the actual connexion of the parts of the electromagnetic field'.[23] The mechanical ether model was a mechanical analogy, linking the concept of the field to a mechanical representation; like the physical analogy of fluid flow which he had employed to represent the theory of lines of force, the physical model provided an embodiment of a mathematical representation, not a depiction of physical reality.

§4. Dynamical explanation: the problem of hidden structure

Maxwell's concern with the status of his mechanical model of the field, and the relationship between physical and mathematical representation, found expression in his paper on 'A dynamical theory of the electromagnetic field' (1865), a theory of the field grounded on the Lagrangian method of analytical dynamics rather than on the construction of a specific mechanical model to represent the structure of the ether. While he still assumes that 'motion is communicated from one part of the [ethereal] medium to another by forces arising from the connexion of those parts', he now disclaims his earlier description of 'a particular kind of motion and a particular kind of strain, so arranged as to account for the phenomena'.[24]

As Maxwell explains in the *Treatise*, there was in principle no limit to the number of mechanical models which could be proposed as putative hypotheses to exlain the propagation of action in the ether: 'The problem of determining the mechanism required to establish a given species of connexion between the motions of the parts of a system always admits of an infinite number of solutions'.[25] While he abandons the mechanical analogy of a cellular ether, the formulation of a representation of the field is nevertheless constrained by the programme of mechanical or dynamical explanation, for his dynamical theory of the electromagnetic field assumes that electromagnetic phenomena were produced by the motions of particles of matter, that action was transmitted in the field by 'a complicated mechanism capable of a vast variety of motion'. Abandoning any attempt to elaborate a specific model to describe this mechanism, he continues to employ mechanical terms which 'will assist [the reader] in understanding electrical [phenomena]', the use of these mechanical correlates of electromagnetic quantities being 'considered as illustrative, not as explanatory', highlighting the dynamical framework of the theory of the field.[26]

The dynamical framework of the theory appears clearly in Maxwell's emphasis on the field as a repository of energy. Maintaining that energy could only exist in connection with material substances, he concludes that the ethereal medium which constituted the field was the repository of the energy of the electromagnetic field. The complicated mechanism of the ether was subject to the laws of dynamics, and the field was represented dynamically in terms of energy transformations in the ether. While the use of mechanical correlates for electromagnetic quantities was merely illustrative, Maxwell declares that 'in speaking of the Energy of the field, however, I wish to be understood literally'. Because 'all energy is the same as mechanical energy' the energy in electromagnetic phenomena was to be referred to the kinetic energy of motion of the parts of the ether and the potential energy stored up in the connections of the mechanical structure of the ether. The propagation of electromagnetic action 'consists in the continual transformation of one of these forms of energy into the other alternately'. The mechanism of the field is thus explicated in terms of the dynamical theory of energy transformations.[27]

In his *Treatise on Electricity and Magnetism* (1873) Maxwell develops this dynamical interpretation of the field in terms of the analytical formulation of dynamics as articulated by Thomson and Tait in their *Treatise on Natural Philosophy* (1867). Maxwell represents Lagrange's method as a formulation of generalised equations of motion considered as 'pure algebraical quantities' in a manner 'free from the intrusion of dynamical ideas', a purely mathematical formalism that avoided reference to the concepts of momentum, velocity and energy after they had been replaced by symbols in the generalised equations of motion. Maxwell by contrast aims to follow Thomson and Tait in seeking 'to cultivate our dynamical ideas'.[28]

The basic mathematical axiom in Thomson and Tait's treatment of dynamics was a theorem discovered by Thomson, which related the variation of a system by impulsive forces (which act in an infinitesimal time-increment) to the kinetic energy of the system, enabling generalised equations of motion to be derived from the supposition of impulsive forces.[29] By grounding the mathematical argument on the concept of impulsive forces, Maxwell argues that this method 'kept out of view the mechanism by which the parts of the system are connected' while keeping 'constantly in mind the ideas appropriate to the fundamental science of dynamics', the dynamical concepts appropriate to the representation of physical reality. The method avoided explicit consideration of the mechanical connections and forces of the electromagnetic field 'because we can eliminate these forces from the equations of motion by the method given by Lagrange for any connected system', while at the same time expressing the 'dynamical ideas from a physical point of view'.

This method satisfied Maxwell's criterion for the acceptability of mathematical methods in natural philosophy, that any mathematical formalism must keep the physical problem clearly in focus. As in his use of the physical analogy of fluid flow to represent the spatial distribution of lines of force, where the geometrical model of fluid flow provided a physical embodiment of lines of force, Maxwell's dynamical theory of the field emphasises the link between the mathematical formalism and the physical reality depicted, ensuring that 'we must have our minds imbued with these dynamical truths as well as with mathematical methods'.[30]

In the *Treatise* Maxwell declares that he had aimed to form a 'mental representation' of the action of the ethereal medium constituting the electromagnetic field. He argues that any physical theory must embody what he terms a 'consistent representation' of the phenomena, an expression he derived from a remark by Gauss on the need to form a 'constructible representation [*construirbare Vorstellung*]' of the manner in which the propagation of electric action takes place. Maxwell seeks to emphasise the need to formulate a physical representation of the field which would be consistent both with dynamical principles and physical phenomena. In emphasising that the functional formalism of his dynamical theory was grounded on physical principles, Maxwell maintains that the *Treatise* provides a symbolic representation which is explicated in terms of dynamical principles, while avoiding the supposition of any theory about the structure of matter constituting the field.[31] The embodiment of a generalised formalism by a dynamical interpretation fulfilled Maxwell's criterion for theory construction: 'We therefore avail ourselves of the labours of the mathematicians, and retranslate their results from the language of the calculus into the language of dynamics, so that our words may call up the mental image, not of some algebraical process, but of some property of moving bodies'.[32]

§5. Mechanical explanation and the analogy of nature

Despite the power of the dynamical method in providing a physical interpretation of a symbolic representation, Maxwell remained dissatisfied with this method of dynamical explanation. He emphasises that according to the theory of the *Treatise* electrical action was 'a phenomenon due to an unknown cause, subject only to the general laws of dynamics', but that a 'complete dynamical theory' of the electromagnetic field would represent the hidden structure of the material system constituting the field, so that 'the whole intermediate mechanism and details of the motion, are taken as the object of study'. Although he realised that an infinite number of mechanical ether models could be constructed so as to represent the field, his desire to achieve a 'complete' theory of the field explicated in terms of 'known motions of known portions of matter' led him to envisage the possiblity of constructing a mechanical model fully consistent with physical reality.[33]

The supposition of a mechanical model of the field based upon a hidden structure of particles of matter raised an important epistemological problem: on what basis could properties be ascribed to the unobservable substratum of particles whose motions constituted the field? Maxwell discussed this question in the *Treatise* as well as in various essays, reviews and unpublished manuscripts written in the 1870s. In the *Treatise* he points out that field theory is based on the supposition of 'intermediate connexions' between distant bodies explicated in terms of 'internal forces' between the particles constituting the field. Hence 'the observed action at a considerable distance is therefore explained by means of a great number of forces acting between bodies at very small distances, for which we are as little able to account as for the action at any distance however great'. Maxwell thus recognises that to replace forces acting between sensible bodies across large distances by internal forces acting between insensible particles across small distances would be to replace one unknown by another. Nevertheless he maintains that 'by establishing the necessity of assuming these internal forces . . . we have advanced a step . . . which will not be lost, though we should fail in accounting for these internal forces, or in explaining the mechanism by which they can be maintained'.[34]

Maxwell clearly recognises the problematic status of any theory of the hidden structure of the mechanism constituting the field. The explanation of the mode of action of the internal forces remained in question. However he emphasises that he considered the 'next step' to be important, 'to account by mechanical considerations' for the internal forces in the electromagnetic ether. He adds that 'I therefore leave the theory at this point'.[35] The implication, in the *Treatise*, is that the internal forces should be explicated in terms of a mechanical model, for he emphasises that the programme of achieving a 'complete dynamical theory' of the field assumed that the intermediate connections of the hidden mechanism constituting the field could be represented by a mechanical model. This programme of mechanical representation assumed that the properties of the particles and the internal forces of the unobservable substratum of the field were analogous to the properties of mechanisms of wheels and gears. Thus Maxwell's physical model of lines of force in 1861 was based on a mechanical analogy between the rotation of vortices and the gearing mechanism employed in machines. But in various writings in the 1870s Maxwell questioned the analogy between molecules and 'internal forces' and the properties of observable particles of matter.

Maxwell's concern with the nature of matter and molecular forces arose from his work on the theory of gases where he was led to consider collisions and encounters between gas molecules.[36] In connection with this problem, in his 'Dynamical theory of gases' (1867) he developed a mathematical model which represented molecular collisions not in terms of impacts between solid, extended particles, but as 'encounters' between molecules considered as 'mere points, or pure centres of force endowed with inertia'. He goes on to declare that 'the doctrines that all matter is extended, and that no two portions of matter can coincide in the same place, being deductions from our experiments with bodies sensible to us, have no application to the theory of molecules'.[37] He develops this point further in his essay on 'Atom' (1875): the assumption that two atoms could not coincide 'seems an unwarrantable concession to the vulgar opinion that two bodies cannot co-exist in the same place. This opinion is deduced from our experience of the behaviour of bodies of sensible size, but we have no experimental evidence that two atoms may not sometimes coincide'.[38] Maxwell therefore explicitly contests the assumption that properties of atoms and molecules can be inferred from the properties of observable particles of matter.

In questioning the doctrine that unobservable atoms and molecules possessed the property of extension, and in refusing to ascribe impenetrability to atoms, Maxwell was implicitly denying Newton's third rule of philosophising, the principle that the 'analogy of nature' enabled certain essential properties (including extension and impenetrability) which were perceived in sensible bodies to be ascribed universally to all bodies in nature, including unobservable atoms. Maxwell regards this Newtonian metaphysical principle as philosophically vulgar. Based on an appeal to sensory experience the Newtonian doctrine of the 'analogy of nature' claims explicitly to characterise the properties of an invisible realm of atoms which are in principle beyond the evidence of experience. Maxwell therefore concludes that there are no good grounds for asserting that atoms and molecules are extended, impenetrable entities.

There can be little doubt that Maxwell, philosophically sophisticated and notably well read, was perfectly aware of the Newtonian pedigree of the doctrine he was disparaging. Newton's 'analogy of nature' was the subject of some discussion among Maxwell's older Cambridge contemporaries. James Challis supported his general theory of physics and molecular forces by an appeal to Newton's 'foundation of all philosophy', declaring that 'the experience of the *senses* relative to masses is necessary and sufficient for revealing to us the universal properties of the ultimate constituents of the masses'.[39] In a letter to Maxwell in 1861, occasioned by Maxwell's comments on his theories and his own published reply, Challis told Maxwell that his own theories were 'strictly within the rules of the Newtonian principles of Philosophy'.[40] By contrast, in his *Philosophy of the Inductive Sciences* (1840, 2nd ed. 1847) which Maxwell had read,[41] William Whewell had regarded the third rule of philosophising as 'a mode of reasoning far from conclusive'. Whewell argued that the assumption that atoms possessed properties of hardness and solidity was

> an incongruous and untenable appendage to the Newtonian view of the Atomic Theory . . . [for] if the hardness *of the bodies* depends upon the . . . [hardness] of the particles, upon what does the hardness *of the particles* depend? What progress do we make in explaining the properties of bodies, when we assume the same properties in our explanation? and to what purpose do we assume that the particles *are* hard?[42]

The assumption of the hardness and impenetrability of atoms was unwarranted by experience, and in any case provided no basis for the explanation of the hardness and impenetrability of sensible bodies.

In implicitly denying the 'analogy of nature' Maxwell thus distinguishes between the laws applicable to sensible bodies and those applicable to the invisible substratum of atoms. In an unpublished essay on 'Science and free will' (1873) he states that 'a constituent molecule of a body has properties very different from those of the body to which it belongs', emphasising the disjunction between sensible and insensible particles.[43] In an unpublished manuscript he developed this issue further:

> when we come to deal with very small quantities of matter its properties begin to be different from those observed in large massses . . . the forces which we call molecular begin to show themselves acting in a different manner from those forces which are alone sensible in their action on great masses. There is therefore a real distinction between very small and very large bodies in nature.[44]

Maxwell here indicates the implication of his rejection of the 'analogy of nature' and his emphatic disjunction between observable and unobservable particles for his discussion of 'internal forces' in the *Treatise*. The formulation of a mechanical analogy of the field, to provide a complete explanation of the hidden structure of the field, assumed the possibility of explaining the properties of the molecules constituting the field by analogy with the mechanical properties of observable particles of matter. Yet in questioning the assumption that atoms and molecules possessed properties of extension and impenetrability, and in emphasising the disjunction between molecular forces and the forces between sensible particles of matter,

Maxwell rejected the 'analogy of nature' which established the intelligibility of formulating a mechanical analogy of the unobservable particles constituting the hidden structure of the field. The formulation of 'complete dynamical theory' of the 'intermediate mechanism' of the field was therefore in conflict with Maxwell's construal of the limitations of analogical argument. The nature of the 'internal forces' between the unobservable particles remained unknown. But the precise virtue of the dynamical formalism was that the 'nature and laws' of the internal forces could remain unspecified because 'we can eliminate these forces from the equations of motion by the method given by Lagrange for any connected system'.[45]

In a review of the second edition of Thomson and Tait's *Treatise on Natural Philosophy* (1879) Maxwell argues that the dynamical method avoided consideration of the nature of the material substratum of the field because the basic concepts of dynamics were defined in a manner which was strictly independent of any speculations about the defining properties of the material substratum of physical reality. Maxwell declares that the dynamical method avoids consideration of 'the relation of mass, as defined in dynamics, to the matter which constitutes real bodies'. The problem as to whether 'real bodies may or may not have such a substratum [of matter]' is simply not a question which is raised by the dynamical method.

The conceptual rationale of the dynamical method is grounded on the disjunction between the dynamical concept of mass and the notion of matter as the material substratum of bodies. Within the dynamical formalism mass, the 'dynamical' concept of 'matter', is not conceived as a substantial reality but is regarded as a mathematical entity: 'what we sometimes, even in abstract dynamics, call matter, is not that unknown substratum of real bodies, against which Berkeley directed his arguments, but something as perfectly intelligible as a straight line or a sphere'.[46] Maxwell here alludes to Berkeley's critique of the ascription of primary qualities of extension and solidity to the unobservable corpuscles which natural philosophers such as Boyle and Newton had postulated as the constituents of material reality. Maxwell's point is that the notion of matter as the material substratum of bodies is not considered in the formalism of the dynamical method. As he remarks in the

Treatise, the 'fundamental dynamical idea of matter' is that matter is 'the recipient of momentum and of energy'.[47]

The thrust of Maxwell's metaphysical explication of the conceptual foundations of the dynamical method is the disjunction between the nature of substances and the framework of dynamical principles. There is therefore a marked contrast between Maxwell's account of the conceptual foundations of his theory of dynamics and Newton's discussion of the ontological status of the laws of motion of *Principia*. While Newton had argued that the conceptual status of force was defined by the mathematical formalism of *Principia*, the intelligibility of his concept of force is grounded on the disjunction between force and inertia, inertia being defined as an essential property of matter. The nature of material substance is therefore crucial to the rationale of Newton's mechanics. By contrast, Maxwell's theory of dynamical explanation is based on the argument that inertia, conceived as a dynamical concept, is not defined as an inherent property of matter. Maxwell rejects the 'Manichaean doctrine of the innate depravity of matter [conceived as a dynamical entity]', and dismisses the assumption that ' "matter" [as a dynamical entity] has any power, either innate or acquired of resisting external influences'.

Maxwell underlines his refusal to ground dynamics on the concept of substance by rejecting the claim that the Newtonian concept of the inherent passivity and inertia of matter defined the dynamical concept of matter. According to Maxwell's exposition of his dynamical principles matter, conceived as a substantial entity, is not a dynamical concept. The dynamical formalism is grounded on the concept of mass, the dynamical concept of matter:

> Whatever may be our opinion about the relation of mass, as defined in dynamics, to the matter which constitutes real bodies, the practical interest of the science [of dynamics] arises from the fact that real bodies *do* behave in a manner strikingly analogous to that in which we have proved that the mass-systems of abstract dynamics *must* behave.[48]

§6. Substantial and functional representation

Maxwell's discussion of conceptual foundations highlights the importance of the relation between substantial and functional representation. His argument is especially significant in that he seeks not simply to assert the sufficiency of a purely symbolic or functional mode of representation, grounded on dynamical principles, but that he explicates this interpretation of his theory of dynamics by an appeal to metaphysical principles. By a rigorous analysis of ontological issues, the nature of matter as the substratum of bodies, the status of the 'analogy of nature', and the relation between dynamical and substantial concepts, Maxwell seeks to establish the conceptual rationale of his dynamics by an appeal to metaphysical argument. In seeking a clear and consistent interpretation of dynamical principles Maxwell seeks to clarify the status of the concept of matter in physical theory, distinguishing between the concept of matter as the material substratum (the substantial concept of matter) and the concept of matter as a dynamical entity (a functional concept of matter). Maxwell's arguments thus attest to the continued significance of the tradition of natural philosophy which has been the concern of this book, a tradition concerned to explicate the metaphysical foundations of physical theory by an analysis of the status of the concept of substance in the foundations of physics.

In the 1880s and 1890s Maxwell's method of 'dynamical theory' was employed by physicists in developing field and ether theories. As Joseph Larmor observed in his 'Dynamical theory of the electric and luminiferous medium' (1893), the aim of the method was to establish a formal statement of the distribution of energy in the electromagnetic field without entering into speculation about the physical properties of the 'primordial medium which is assumed to be the ultimate seat of all phenomena'. The dynamical theory of the field as interpreted by Maxwell involved no necessary assumption of ontological correlates:

> The precise force of Lagrange's method, in its physical application [by Maxwell], consists in its allowing us to ignore or leave out of account altogether the details of the mechanism, whatever it is, that is in operation in the phenomena under discussion; it makes everything depend on a single analytical function representing the distribution of energy in the medium in terms of suitable coordinates of position and of their velocities; from the location of this energy, its subsequent play and the dynamical phenomena involved in it are all deducible by straightforward mathematical analysis.[49]

The relationship between the functional dynamical formalism and the problem of substance remained for Maxwell as a
fundamental problem requiring analysis. In a letter to Tait in
1867 Maxwell refers to Berkeley's discussion of the nature of
matter. Maxwell wrote that: 'Matter is *never* perceived by the
senses. According to Torricelli quoted by Berkeley "Matter is
nothing but an enchanted vase of Circe, fitted to receive
Impulse and Energy, essences so subtle that nothing but the
inmost nature of material substance is able to contain them"'.[50]
Matter as the substratum of real bodies is therefore unknowable,
and the dynamical theory of nature is not grounded on the
supposition of a substratum of matter but on the 'fundamental
dynamical idea of matter, as capable by its motion of becoming
the recipient of momentum and of energy'.[51] Maxwell quotes
directly from Torricelli in the closing paragraph of the *Treatise*:
'energy, as Torricelli remarked, "is a quintessence of so subtle a
nature that it cannot be contained in every vessel except the
inmost substance of material things"'. While the dynamical
theory of the field is concerned with the distribution of energy in
the field, energy cannot be conceived independently of 'a
medium or substance in which the energy exists'.

The basis of the field approach is not to specify the nature of
the substratum of matter, but rather to represent the 'dynamical' idea of matter as the recipient of energy, and hence to
'construct a mental representation' of the 'conception of a
medium in which the propagation [of energy] takes place' in
terms of the dynamical theory of matter as the recipient of
energy. Maxwell's 'consistent representation' of the transmission of energy in the field is therefore elaborated in terms of
the dynamical theory of matter. He declares that 'this has been
my constant aim in this treatise'.[52]

The attempt to construct a representation of the mode of
action of the material system of the field, envisaged in terms of
the dynamical idea of matter as the receptacle of energy, rather
than in terms of the internal forces between the hidden structure
of the primordial substratum of matter *qua* substance, expresses
Maxwell's aim of formulating a 'consistent representation' of
the field. While matter *qua* substratum is unknowable, the
method of dynamical explanation provides the basis for a
physical interpretation of a symbolic representation, based on

the disjunction between dynamical (functional) and substantial representations of matter. Maxwell thus seeks to resolve the problem of substance.

Notes

[1] James Clerk Maxwell, *A Treatise on Electricity and Magnetism*, 2 vols. (Oxford, 1873), Vol. 2, p. 183.

[2] J. C. Maxwell, 'On action at a distance' [1873], *The Scientific Papers of James Clerk Maxwell*, 2 vols., ed. W. D. Niven (Cambridge, 1890), Vol. 2, pp. 312, 316. *Cf.* C. Maclaurin, *An Account of Sir Isaac Newton's Philosophical Discoveries* (London, 1748), pp. 109–11.

[3] J. C. Maxwell, 'A dynamical theory of the electromagnetic field' [1865], *Papers*, Vol. 1, pp. 527, 533. On Maxwell's contribution to the development of the field concept see M. B. Hesse, *Forces and Fields* (London, 1961), pp. 189–225; and P. M. Harman, *Energy, Force, and Matter* (Cambridge, 1982), pp. 72–3, 84–98.

[4] For a full discussion of Maxwell's development of Faraday's concepts see P. M. Heimann, 'Maxwell and the modes of consistent representation', *Arch. Hist. Exact Sci.*, 6 (1970), 171–213.

[5] J. C. Maxwell, 'On Faraday's lines of force' [1856], *Papers*, Vol. 1, pp. 158, 160.

[6] W. Thomson, 'On the uniform motion of heat in homogeneous bodies, and its connection with the mathematical theory of electricity', *Camb. Math. J.*, 3 (1842), 71–84.

[7] Maxwell to Thomson, 13 September 1855, in J. Larmor, *The Origins of Clerk Maxwell's Electric Ideas as Described in Familiar Letters to William Thomson* (Cambridge, 1937), p. 17.

[8] Maxwell, *Papers*, Vol. 1, p. 157. Draft of 'Faraday's lines of force', Add. 7655, Cambridge University Library.

[9] Maxwell, *Papers*, Vol. 1, p. 160.

[10] L. Campbell and W. Garnett, *The Life of James Clerk Maxwell* (London, 1882), p. 243. See also G. E. Davie, *The Democratic Intellect*, 2nd ed. (Edinburgh, 1964), pp. 192–6; and R. Olson, *Scottish Philosophy and British Physics 1750–1880* (Princeton, 1975), pp. 287–321.

[11] J. C. Maxwell, *An Elementary Treatise on Electricity*, ed. W. Garnett (Oxford, 1881), p. 52.

[12] Maxwell, *Papers*, Vol. 1, pp. 155–6.

[13] Draft of 'Faraday's lines of force' (see note 8 above); Maxwell, *Papers*, Vol. 1, p. 158.

[14] Maxwell, *Treatise*, Vol. 2, p. 164.

[15] Maxwell to Faraday, 9 November 1857, in L. Campbell and W. Garnett, *The Life of James Clerk Maxwell*, 2nd ed. (London, 1884), p. 203. Maxwell was responding to Faraday's essay 'On the conservation of force', *Phil. Mag.*, 13 (1857), 225–39.

[16] Maxwell, *Papers*, Vol. 1, p. 188. Maxwell was referring to W. Thomson, 'On a mechanical representation of electric, magnetic and galvanic forces'

[1847], *Mathematical and Physical Papers*, 6 vols. (Cambridge, 1882–1911), Vol. 1, pp. 76–80.

17 Campbell and Garnett, *Life of Maxwell*, 2nd ed., p. 204. Maxwell was referring to W. Thomson, 'Dynamical illustrations of the magnetic and heliocoidal rotary effects of transparent bodies on polarised light', *Proc. Roy. Soc.*, 8 (1856), 150–8.

18 J. C. Maxwell, 'Oh physical lines of force' [1861/2], *Papers*, Vol. 1, pp. 452, 489, 468. See also D. M. Siegel, 'Thomson, Maxwell and the universal ether in Victorian physics' in *Conceptions of Ether*, ed. G. N. Cantor and M. J. S. Hodge (Cambridge, 1981), pp. 239–68; and M. J. Klein, 'Mechanical explanation at the end of the nineteenth century', *Centaurus*, 17 (1972), 58–82.

19 Maxwell, *Papers*, Vol. 1, p. 486; *idem, Treatise*, Vol. 2, p. 416.

20 P. M. Harman, *Energy, Force, and Matter*, pp. 79–84.

21 Maxwell, *Papers*, Vol. 1, p. 500.

22 C. G. Knott, *Life and Scientific Work of Peter Guthrie Tait* (Cambridge, 1911), p. 215.

23 Maxwell, *Treatise*, Vol. 2, pp. 416–17.

24 Maxwell, *Papers*, Vol. 1, pp. 532–3, 563.

25 Maxwell, *Treatise*, Vol. 2, p. 417.

26 Maxwell, *Papers'*, Vol. 1, pp. 533, 564.

27 Maxwell, *Papers*, Vol. 1, pp. 529, 564.

28 Maxwell, *Treatise*, Vol. 2, pp. 184–5.

29 *Cf* D. F. Moyer, 'Energy, dynamics, hidden machinery', *Stud. Hist. Phil. Sci.*, 8 (1977) 251–68.

30 Maxwell, *Treatise*, Vol. 2, pp. 183–4, 193–4.

31 Maxwell, *Treatise*, Vol. 2, pp. 435, 438; C. F. Gauss, *Werke*, 12 vols. (Göttingen, 1863–1933), Vol. 5, p. 629. *Cf.* Olson, *Scottish Philosophy and British Physics*, pp. 312–16.

32 Maxwell, *Treatise*, Vol. 2, p. 185.

33 Maxwell, *Treatise*, Vol. 2, p. 202.

34 Maxwell, *Treatise*, Vol. 1, pp. 122–3, 127.

35 Maxwell, *Treatise*, Vol. 1, p. 132.

36 S. G. Brush, *The Kind of Motion We Call Heat*, 2 vols. (Amsterdam, 1976). Vol. 1, pp. 160–230.

37 Maxwell, 'On the dynamical theory of gases' [1867], *Papers*, Vol. 2, p. 33.

38 Maxwell, 'Atom' [1875], *Papers*, Vol. 2, p. 448.

39 J. Challis, 'On Newton's "Foundation of all Philosophy"', *Phil. Mag.*, 26 (1863), 282.

40 Challis to Maxwell, 10 June 1861, Add. 7655, Cambridge University Library. *Cf.* Maxwell, 'On physical lines of force', *Phil. Mag.*, 21 (1861), 163, and J. Challis, 'On theories of magnetism and other forces, in reply to remarks by Professor Maxwell', *Phil. Mag.*, 21 (1861), 250–4.

41 *Cf.* Maxwell to R. B. Litchfield, 6 June 1855 and 4 July 1856, Campbell and Garnett, *Life of Maxwell*, pp. 215, 261.

42 W. Whewell, *Philosophy of the Inductive Sciences*, 2nd ed., 2 vols. (London, 1847), Vol. 2, p. 289; Vol. 1, p. 432.

43 Campbell and Garnett, *Life of Maxwell*, p. 439.

44 Maxwell, 'Dimensions of physical quantities', Add. 7655, Cambridge University Library.

45 Maxwell, *Treatise*, Vol. 2, pp. 183, 202.

46 Maxwell, 'Thomson and Tait's Natural Philosophy' [1879], *Papers*, Vol. 2, p. 781. *Cf.* T. K. Simpson, 'Some observations on Maxwell's *Treatise on Electricity and Magnetism*', *Stud. Hist. Phil. Sci.*, 1 (1970), 249–63.

47 Maxwell, *Treatise*, Vol. 2, p. 181.

48 Maxwell, *Papers*, Vol. 2, pp. 779, 781.

49 J. Larmor, 'A dynamical theory of the electric and luminiferous medium' [1893], *Mathematical and Physical Papers*, 2 vols. (Cambridge, 1929), Vol. 1, p. 389.

50 Knott, *Life of Tait*, p. 195. See George Berkeley, *De motu* [1721], *Works*, 9 vols., ed., A. A. Luce and T. E. Jessop (London, 1948–57), Vol. 4, p. 13, where Berkeley wrote 'force' for Maxwell's 'energy'. See also E. Torricelli, *Lezioni Accademiche* [1715], *Opere*, 4 vols., ed., G. Loria and G. Vassura (Faenza, 1919–44), Vol. 2, p. 27.

51 Maxwell, *Treatise*, Vol. 2, p. 181.

52 Maxwell, *Treatise*, Vol. 2, p. 438.

CHAPTER VIII

Conclusion

> That matter, as such, should have certain fundamental properties, that it should have a continuous existence in space and time, that all action should be between two portions of matter, and so on, are truths which may, for aught we know, be of the kind which metaphysicians call necessary. We may use our knowledge of such truths for purposes of deduction, but we have no data for speculating on their origin.[1]

Commenting on the theory of matter in his article on 'Atom' (1875) Maxwell emphasised that discussion of the nature of substance could not be conducted simply by appeal to empirical data and laws but required reference to metaphysical argument. The main theme of this book has been the status of the problem of substance in 'classical' physics and the consequent appeal by natural philosophers to metaphysical foundations. In providing historical examples of the provision of metaphysical foundations, this study has aimed to support the interpretation of the structure of scientific argument which maintains that the articulation of scientific theories rests on metaphysical as well as empirical constraints.[2]

In exploring the metaphysical and ontological foundations of some of the systems of natural philosophy comprising 'classical' physics this study has highlighted the appeal by natural philosophers to metaphysical argument to explicate the status of mathematical and physical representations of nature. Thus, Newton distinguished between a physico-mathematical representation of force and the metaphysical issues surrounding the ontological status and causal agency of forces. While Leibniz stressed the metaphysical foundations of his dynamics and its basis in his theory of substance, his theory of physical representation is based on the supposition of the sufficiency and phenomenal status of his physics of derivative forces *qua* scientific explanations. Maxwell emphasised the disjunction between a mathematical formalism and a physical hypothesis, a distinction that is basic to his construal of the role of mechanical analogies and his explication of the conceptual status of matter as a mathematical entity rather than a substantial reality, which established the rationale of his method of dynamical explanation. These natural philosophers were concerned to explicate the relation between functional and substantial representation and to clarify the different levels of explanation in natural philosophy by appeal to metaphysical argument.

The problem of substance and the consequent appeal to metaphysical argument is therefore basic to the conceptual structure of 'classical' physics. Natural philosophers appealed to metaphysical foundations in an attempt to justify the intelligibility of their basic assumptions about physical reality. Kant's discussion of metaphysical foundations provides a clear exposition of the metaphysical assumptions underlying Newton's physical principles. Kant seeks to establish Newton's physical laws by reappraising the metaphysical foundations of Newton's concept of gravitation and laws of motion. By appeal to metaphysical argument Faraday sought to refute the postulates of atomism, and to justify his theory of the spatial disposition of forces in the field by grounding his concept of force on a theory of material substance, arguing that matter filled space by its inherent forces. Similarly, Helmholtz sought to demonstrate the intelligibility of his mechanistic ontology which established the rationale of his energy physics by appeal to Kant's metaphysics of nature. Metaphysical argument thus served to establish the intelligibility and conceptual rationale of physical theories.

The systems of natural philosophy discussed in this book have demonstrated the importance of a cluster of concepts in the development of 'classical' physics. The status of the concepts of force and inertia; the intelligibility of action at a distance (and the appeal to a theory of the mediation of forces in an ambient field); the problem of the activity and passivity of matter; and the status of the problem of substance, were issues which dominated debate. While these problems received an authoritative statement in Newton's work, in a way which shaped the development of subsequent natural philosophy, the ontology of Newtonian physics was the subject of considerable dispute. It is apparent that the systems of natural philosophy comprising 'classical' physics display considerable ontological diversity. Concepts of force, matter, field and energy did not have a unique meaning in classical physics. Understanding 'classical' physics requires the explanation of the relations between, and the meaning of, the entities posited by these ontologies.[3] To achieve this task natural philosophers sought to explicate metaphysical foundations.

This historical study thus has a bearing on the discussion of the epistemological status of scientific discourse. The instrumentalist view of science, that theories function as symbolic representations of the data of experience, merely describes the functional level of scientific argument. Nor does the empiricist view of scientific realism, that the reality of physical entities is validated by empirical evidence, satisfactorily describe the explanatory structure of theoretical discourses. Metaphysical arguments, the appeal to regulative maxims of causality or analogy, and the explication of the intelligibility of concepts, play a crucial role in the articulation of scientific theories. The recognition that the conceptual framework of an ontology is supported by appeal to metaphysical foundations constitutes an enrichment of our understanding of the structure of scientific discourse.

Notes

[1] J. C. Maxwell, 'Atom' [1875], *Scientific Papers*, Vol. 2, p. 482.

[2] G. Buchdahl, 'Neo-transcendental approaches towards scientific theory appraisal', in *Science, Belief and Behaviour*, ed. D. H. Mellor (Cambridge, 1980), pp. 1–21. *Cf.* J. Mittelstrass, 'The Galilean revolution', *Stud. Hist. Phil. Sci.*, 2 (1972), 297–328.

[3] *Cf.* S. Gaukroger, *Explanatory Structures* (Hassocks, 1978), pp. 39–57.

Bibliography

Adickes, Erich, *Kant als Naturforscher*, 2 vols. (Berlin, 1924–5).

Aiton, E. J., *The Vortex Theory of Planetary Motions* (London/New York, 1972).

Berkeley, George, *The Works of George Berkeley*, ed. A. A. Luce and T. E. Jessop, 9 vols. (London, 1948–57).

Bernoulli, Johann, 'Discours sur les loix de la communication du mouvement' [1727], *Recueil des pieces qui a remporté les prix de l'Académie Royale des Sciences, Tome premier* (Paris, 1732).

————, 'Theoremata selecta, pro conservatione virium vivarum demonstranda', *Commentarii Academiae Scientiarum Imperialis Petropolitanae*, 2 (1727), 200–7.

————, 'Meditationes de chordis vibrantibus', *Commentarii Academiae Petropolitanae*, 3 (1728), 13–28.

————, 'De vera notione virium vivarum earumque usu in dynamicis', *Acta Eruditorum*, (1735), 210–30.

————, *Opera Omnia, tam antea sparsim edita, quam hactenus inedita*, 4 vols. (Lausanne/Geneva, 1742).

Boerhaave, Herman, *A New Method of Chemistry: Including the History, Theory and Practice of the Art: Translated from the Original Latin of Dr. Boerhaave's Elementa Chemiae*, 2 vols., trans. P. Shaw (London, 1741).

Boscovich, R. J., *A Theory of Natural Philosophy*, Venetian ed. of 1763 trans. J. M. Child (London, 1922).

Boyle, Robert, *The Origine of Formes and Qualities, Considered According to the Corpuscular Philosophy* (Oxford, 1666).

Brittan, Gordon G., *Kant's Theory of Science* (Princeton, 1978).

Brush, Stephen G., *The Kind of Motion We Call Heat. A History of the Kinetic Theory of Gases in the Nineteenth Century*, 2 vols. (Amsterdam, 1976).

Buchdahl, Gerd, *Metaphysics and the Philosophy of Science. The Classical Origins: Descartes to Kant* (Oxford, 1969).

————, 'Gravity and intelligibility: Newton to Kant', in *The Methodological Heritage of Newton*, ed. R. E. Butts and J. W. Davis (Oxford, 1970), pp. 74–102.

————, 'History of science and criteria of choice', in *Historical and Philosophical Perspectives of Science*, ed. R. H. Stuewer (Minneapolis, 1970), pp. 204–30.

————, 'The conception of lawlikeness in Kant's philosophy of science', *Synthese*, 23 (1971), 24–46.

————, 'Explanation and gravity', in *Changing Perspectives in the History of*

Science, ed. M. Teich and R. M. Young (London, 1973), pp. 167–203.

————, 'Neo-transcendental approaches towards scientific theory appraisal', in *Science, Belief and Behaviour*, ed. D. H. Mellor (Cambridge, 1980), pp. 1–21.

Burtt, E. A., *The Metaphysical Foundations of Modern Physical Science*, 2nd ed. (London, 1932).

Butts, R. E. and Davis, J. W. (eds.), *The Methodological Heritage of Newton* (Oxford/Toronto, 1970).

Calinger, Ronald S., 'The Newtonian-Wolffian confrontation in the St. Petersburg Academy of Sciences (1725–1746)', *Journal of World History*, 11 (1968), 417–35.

————, 'The Newtonian-Wolffian controversy', *Journal of the History of Ideas*, 30 (1969), 319–30.

Campbell, L. and Garnett, W., *The Life of James Clerk Maxwell* (London, 1882); 2nd ed. (London, 1884).

Cantor, G. N. and Hodge, M. J. S. (eds.), *Conceptions of Ether: Studies in the History of Ether Theories 1740–1900* (Cambridge, 1981).

Cassirer, Ernst, *The Philosophy of Symbolic Forms. Volume Three: The Phenomenology of Knowledge* (New Haven/London, 1957).

Challis, James, 'On theories of magnetism and other forces, in reply to remarks by Professor Maxwell', *Philosophical Magazine*, 21 (1861), 250–4.

————, 'On Newton's "Foundation of all Philosophy"', *Philosophical Magazine*, 26 (1863), 280–92.

Cohen, I. Bernard, '*Quantum in se est*: Newton's concept of inertia in relation to Descartes and Lucretius', *Notes and Records of the Royal Society of London*, 19 (1964), 131–55.

————, *The Newtonian Revolution* (Cambridge, 1980).

Costabel, Pierre, *Leibniz et la dynamique. Les textes de 1692* (Paris, 1960).

Cranefield, Paul F., 'The organic physics of 1847 and the biophysics of today', *Journal of the History of Medicine*, 12 (1957), 407–23.

Davie, George Elder, *The Democratic Intellect. Scotland and Her Universities in the Nineteenth Century*, 2nd ed. (Edinburgh, 1964).

Descartes, René, *Oeuvres de Descartes*, ed. C. Adam and P. Tannery, 13 vols. (Paris, 1897–1913).

Dijksterhuis, E. J., *The Mechanization of the World Picture*, trans. C. Dikshoorn (London, 1961).

Ecole, Jean, 'Cosmologie wolffienne et dynamique leibnizienne', *Etudes philosophiques*, 19 (1964), 3–10.

Ellington, James, 'The unity of Kant's thought in his philosophy of corporeal nature' in I. Kant, *Metaphysical Foundations of Natural Science*, trans. J. Ellington (Indianapolis/New York, 1970), pp. 135–218.

Eneström, G., 'Der Briefwechsel zwischen Leonhard Euler und Johann I Bernoulli', *Bibliotheca Mathematica* (Series III), 4 (1903), 344–88; *ibid.*, 5 (1904), 248–91; *ibid.*, 6 (1905), 16–87.

Euler, Leonard, 'De la force de percussion et de sa véritable mésure', *Mémoires de l'Académie Royale des Sciences de Berlin*, 1 (1745), 21–53.

————, 'Recherches sur l'origine des forces', *Mémoires de l'Académie des Sciences de Berlin*, 6 (1750), 419–47.

————, *Lettres à une princesse d'Allemagne sur divers sujets de physique et de philosophie*, 3 vols. (St Petersburg, 1768–72).

————, *Leonhardi Euleri Opera Omnia*, Second Series, Volume 5, ed. J. O. Fleckenstein (Lausanne, 1957).

————, *Leonhardi Euleri Opera Omnia*, Third Series, Vols. 11 and 12, ed. A. Speiser (Zürich, 1960).

Faraday, Michael, *Experimental Researches in Electricity*, 3 vols. (London, 1839–55).

————, 'An answer to Dr. Hare's letter on certain theoretical opinions', *Philosophical Magazine*, 17 (1840), 262–74.

————, 'A speculation touching electric conduction and the nature of matter', *Philosophical Magazine*, 24 (1844), 136–44.

————, 'Thoughts on ray-vibrations', *Philosophical Magazine*, 28 (1846), 345–50.

————, 'On the physical character of the lines of magnetic force', *Philosophical Magazine*, 3 (1852), 401–28.

————, 'On the conservation of force', *Philosophical Magazine*, 13 (1857), 225–39.

Fourier, J. B. J., *Théorie analytique de la chaleur* (Paris, 1822).

Fox, Robert, 'The rise and fall of Laplacian physics', *Historical Studies in the Physical Sciences*, 4 (1974), 89–136.

Gabbey, Alan, 'Force and inertia in the seventeenth century: Descartes and Newton', in *Descartes: Philosophy, Mathematics and Physics*, ed. S. Gaukroger (Brighton/Totowa, New Jersey, 1980), pp. 230–320.

Galaty, David H., 'The philosophical basis of mid-nineteenth-century German reductionism', *Journal of the History of Medicine*, 29 (1974), 295–316.

Gaukroger, Stephen, *Explanatory Structures: A Study of Concepts of Explanation in Early Physics and Philosophy* (Hassocks, 1978).

————, (ed.), *Descartes: Philosophy, Mathematics and Physics* (Brighton/Totowa, New Jersey, 1980).

Gauss, Carl Friedrich, *Werke*, 12 vols. (Göttingen, 1863–1933).

Gehler, J. S. T., *Gehlers physikalisches Wörterbuch neu bearbeitet von Brandes, Gmelin, Horner, Muncke, Pfaff*, 10 vols. (Leipzig, 1825–44).

Gooding, David C., 'Conceptual and experimental bases of Faraday's denial of electrostatic action at a distance', *Studies in History and Philosophy of Science*, 9 (1978), 117–49.

Guerlac, Henry E., 'Newton's optical aether', *Notes and Records of the Royal Society of London*, 22 (1967), 45–57.

Gueroult, Martial, 'Métaphysique et physique de la force chez Descartes', *Etudes sur Descartes, Spinoza, Malebranche et Leibniz* (Hildesheim/New York, 1970), pp. 85–121.

————, *Leibniz: dynamique et métaphysique* (Paris, 1967).

Hales, Stephen, *Vegetable Staticks* (London, 1727).

Hamilton, William, *Lectures on Metaphysics and Logic*, ed. H. L. Mansel and J. Veitch, 4 vols. (Edinburgh, 1859).

Hankins, Thomas L., 'Eighteenth-century attempts to resolve the *vis viva* controversy', *Isis*, 56 (1965), 281–97.

Hare, Robert, 'A letter to Professor Faraday on certain theoretical opinions', *Philosophical Magazine*, 17 (1840), 44–54.

Harman, P. M., *Energy, Force, and Matter. The Conceptual Development of Nineteenth-Century Physics* (Cambridge, 1982).

Heilbron, J. L., 'The electric field before Faraday', in *Conceptions of Ether*, ed. G. N. Cantor and M. J. S. Hodge (Cambridge, 1981), pp. 187–213.

Heimann [Harman], P. M., 'Maxwell and the modes of consistent representation', *Archive for History of Exact Sciences*, 6 (1970), 171–213.

———, 'Faraday's theories of matter and electricity', *British Journal for History of Science*, 5 (1971), 235–57.

———, 'Helmholtz and Kant: the metaphysical foundations of *Über die Erhaltung der Kraft*', *Studies in History and Philosophy of Science*, 5 (1974), 205–38.

———, 'Mayer's concept of "force": the "axis" of a new science of physics', *Historical Studies in the Physical Sciences*, 7 (1976), 277–96.

———, '"Geometry and nature": Leibniz and Johann Bernoulli's theory of motion', *Centaurus*, 21 (1977), 1–26.

———, 'Ether and imponderables', in *Conceptions of Ether*, ed. G. N. Cantor and M. J. S. Hodge (Cambridge, 1981), pp. 61–83.

Heimann [Harman], P. M., and McGuire, J. E. 'Newtonian forces and Lockean powers: concepts of matter in eighteenth-century thought', *Historical Studies in the Physical Sciences*, 3 (1971), 233–306.

Heimsoeth, Heinz, *Studien zur Philosophie Immanuel Kants I: metaphysische Ursprünge und ontologische Grundlagen*, 2nd ed. (Bonn, 1971).

Helmholtz, Hermann von, 'Bericht über die Theorie der physiologischen Wärmeerscheinungen für 1845', *Fortschritte der Physik in Jahre 1845* (Berlin, 1847), pp. 346–55.

———, 'Ueber den Stoffverbrauch bei der Muskelaction', *Archiv für Anatomie und Physiologie* (1845), 72–83.

———, *Über die Erhaltung der Kraft* (Berlin, 1847).

———, 'Theorie der Wärme', *Fortschritte der Physik in Jahre 1853* (Berlin, 1856), pp. 404–32.

———, *Handbuch der physiologischen Optik*, 3 vols. (Leipzig, 1856–67).

———, 'On the application of the law of the conservation of force to organic nature', *Proceedings of the Royal Institution*, 3 (1861), 347–57.

———, 'Über die Bewegungsgleichungen der Elektricität für ruhende leitende Körper', *Journal für reine und angewandte Mathematik*, 72 (1870), 57–129.

———, *Wissenschaftliche Abhandlungen* 3 vols. (Leipzig, 1882–95).

———, *Selected Writings of Hermann von Helmholtz*, ed. R. Kahl (Middletown, Conn., 1971).

Herivel, John, *The Background to Newton's 'Principia': A Study of Newton's Dynamical Researches in the Years 1664–84* (Oxford, 1965).

Hesse, Mary B., *Forces and Fields: The Concept of Action at a Distance in the History of Physics* (London, 1961).

Hiebert, Erwin, N., *Historical Roots of the Principle of Conservation of Energy* (Madison, Wisc., 1962).

Hofmann, Joseph E., *Leibniz in Paris 1672–1676: His Growth to Mathematical Maturity* (Cambridge, 1974).

Hoppe, Hansgeorg, *Kants Theorie der Physik. Eine Untersuchung über das Opus postumum von Kant* (Frankfurt, 1969).

Hume, David, *A Treatise of Human Nature*, ed. L. A. Selby-Bigge (Oxford, 1888).

———, *An Enquiry into the Human Understanding*, ed. L. A. Selby-Bigge (Oxford, 1902).

Hutton, James, *Dissertations on Different Subjects in Natural Philosophy* (Edinburgh, 1792).

———, *A Dissertation upon the Philosophy of Light, Heat and Fire* (Edinburgh, 1794).

———, *An Investigation of the Principles of Knowledge, and of the Progress of Reason, from Sense to Science and Philosophy*, 3 vols. (Edinburgh, 1794).

Huygens, Christiaan, 'Régles du mouvement dans la recontre des corps', *Philosophical Transactions of the Royal Society of London*, 4 (1669), 925–8.

———, *Horologium oscillatorium sive de motu pendulorum ad horologium aptato demonstrationes geometricae* (Paris, 1673).

———, *Christiani Huygeni Opuscula Posthuma*, ed. B. de Volder and B. Fullenius (Leiden, 1703).

———, *Oeuvres complètes*, 22 vols. (The Hague, 1888–1950).

Iltis, Carolyn, 'Leibniz and the *vis viva* controversy', *Isis*, 62 (1971) 21–35.

———, 'The decline of Cartesianism in mechanics: the Leibnizian-Cartesian debates', *Isis*, 64 (1973), 356–73.

Joule, James Prescott, 'On the calorific effects of magneto-electricity, and on the mechanical value of heat', *Philosophical Magazine*, 23 (1843), 263–76, 347–55, 435–43.

———, *The Scientific Papers of James Prescott Joule*, 2 vols. (London, 1884–7).

Kant, Immanuel, *Gedanken von der wahren Schätzung der lebendigen Kräfte* (Königsberg, 1747).

———, *Metaphysicae cum geometria iunctae usus in philosophia naturali . . . continet Monadologiam physicam* (Königsberg, 1756).

———, *Metaphysische Anfangsgründe der Naturwissenschaft* (Riga, 1786); *Metaphysical Foundations of Natural Science*, trans. J. Ellington (Indianapolis/ New York, 1970).

———, *Kants gesammelte Schriften. Herausgegeben von der Königlich Preussischen Akademie der Wissenschaften*, 24 vols. (Berlin, 1902–38).

———, *The Critique of Judgement*, trans. J. C. Meredith (Oxford, 1928).

———, *Immanuel Kant's Critique of Pure Reason*, trans. N. Kemp Smith (London, 1933).

Klein, Martin J., 'Mechanical explanation at the end of the nineteenth century', *Centaurus*, 17 (1972), 58–82.

Knott, Cargill Gilston, *Life and Scientific Work of Peter Guthrie Tait* (Cambridge, 1911).

Koenigsberger, Leo, *Hermann von Helmholtz*, trans. and abridged F. A. Welby (Oxford, 1906).

Koyré, Alexandre, *Newtonian Studies* (London, 1965).

Koyré, Alexandre and Cohen, I. B. 'Newton and the Leibniz-Clarke correspondence', *Archives Internationales d'Histoire des Sciences*, 15 (1962), 63–126.

Lagrange, Joseph Louis, *Mécanique analytique*, 2 vols. (Paris, 1965).

Larmor, Joseph, 'A dynamical theory of the electric and luminiferous medium', *Proceedings of the Royal Society*, 54 (1893), 438–61.

———, *Mathematical and Physical Papers*, 2 vols. (Cambridge, 1929).

———, *The Origins of Clerk Maxwell's Electric Ideas as Described in Familiar Letters to William Thomson* (Cambridge, 1937). And in *Proceedings of the Cambridge Philosophical Society*, 32 (1936), 695–750.

Laudan, L. L., 'The *vis viva* controversy: a *post-mortem*', *Isis*, 59 (1968), 131–43.

Leibniz, Gottfried Wilhelm, *Theoria motus abstracti* (Mainz, 1671).

———, 'Brevis demonstratio erroris memorabilis Cartesii', *Acta Eruditorum*, 5 (1686), 161–3.

———, 'Réplique à M. l'Abbé D. C[atelan]', *Nouvelles de la République des Lettres*, 9 (1687), 131–44.

———, 'Lettre de M. Leibniz . . . pour servir de réplique à la résponse du R. P. Malebranche', *Nouvelles de la République des Lettres*, 9 (1687), 744–53.

———, 'De primae philosophiae emendatione, et de notione substantiae', *Acta Eruditorum*, 13 (1694), 110–12.

———, 'Specimen dynamicum', *Acta Eruditorum*, 14 (1695), 145–57.

———, *Leibnizens mathematische Schriften*, ed. C. I. Gerhardt, 7 vols. (Berlin/Halle, 1849–63); reprinted (Hildesheim, 1960–1).

———, *Die philosophischen Schriften von G. W. Leibniz*, ed. C. I. Gerhardt, 7 vols. (Berlin, 1875–90); reprinted (Hildesheim, 1960–1).

———, *The Leibniz-Clarke Correspondence*, ed. H. G. Alexander (Manchester, 1956).

———, *Philosophical Papers and Letters*, trans. L. E. Loemker (Dordrecht, 1969).

Lipman, Timothy O., 'Vitalism and reductionism in Liebig's physiological thought', *Isis*, 58 (1967), 167–85.

Locke, John, *An Essay Concerning Human Understanding*, ed. A. S. Pringle-Pattison (Oxford, 1924).

Maclaurin, Colin, *An Account of Sir Isaac Newton's Philosophical Discoveries* (London, 1748).

Mandelbaum, Maurice, *Philosophy, Science and Sense Perception* (Baltimore, 1964).

Mattern, Ruth M., 'Locke on active power and the obscure idea of active power from bodies', *Studies in History and Philosophy of Science*, 11 (1980), 39–77.

Maxwell, James Clerk, 'On Faraday's lines of force', *Transactions of the Cambridge Philosophical Society*, 10 (1856), 27–83.

———, 'On physical lines of force', *Philosophical Magazine*, 21 (1861), 161–75, 281–91, 338–48; *ibid.*, 23 (1862), 12–24, 85–95.

———, 'A dynamical theory of the electromagnetic field', *Philosophical Transactions of the Royal Society of London*, 155 (1865), 459–512.

————, 'On the dynamical theory of gases', *Philosophical Transactions of the Royal Society*, 157 (1867), 49–88.

————, *A Treatise on Electricity and Magnetism*, 2 vols. (Oxford, 1873).

————, 'On action at a distance', *Nature*, 7 (1873), 323–5, 341–3.

————, 'Atom', *Encyclopaedia Britannica*, 9th ed. (1875), Vol. 3, pp. 36–49.

————, *Matter and Motion* (London, 1877).

————, 'Hermann Ludwig Ferdinand Helmholtz', *Nature*, 15 (1877),389–91.

————, 'Thomson and Tait's Natural Philosophy', *Nature*, 20 (1879), 213–16.

————, *An Elementary Treatise on Electricity*, ed. W. Garnett (Oxford, 1881).

————, *The Scientific Papers of James Clerk Maxwell*, ed. W. D. Niven, 2 vols. (Cambridge, 1890).

Mayer, Julius Robert, *Die Mechanik der Wärme in gesammelten Schriften von Robert Mayer*, ed. J. J. Weyrauch (Stuttgart, 1893).

————, *Kleinere Schriften und Briefe von Robert Mayer*, ed. J. J. Weyrauch (Stuttgart, 1893).

McGuire, J. E., 'Body and void and Newton's *De Mundi Systemate*: some new sources', *Archive for History of Exact Sciences*, 3 (1966), 206–48.

————, 'Transmutation and immutability: Newton's doctrine of physical qualities', *Ambix*, 14 (1967), 69–95.

————, 'The origin of Newton's doctrine of essential qualities', *Centaurus*, 12 (1968), 233–60.

————, 'Force, active principles and Newton's invisible realm', *Ambix*, 15 (1968), 154–208.

————, 'Atoms and the "analogy of nature": Newton's third rule of philosophizing', *Studies in History and Philosophy of Science*, 1 (1970), 3–57.

————, '"Labyrinthus continui": Leibniz on substance, activity and matter', in *Motion and Time, Space and Matter*, ed. P. K. Machamer and R. G. Turnbull (Columbus, Ohio, 1976), pp. 290–326.

McMullin, Ernan, *Newton on Matter and Activity* (Notre Dame/London, 1978).

Meyerson, Emile, *Identity and Reality*, trans. K. Loewenberg (London, 1930).

Mittelstrass, Jürgen, *Neuzeit und Aufklärung: Studien zur Entstehung der neuzeitlichen Wissenschaft und Philosophie* (Berlin/New York, 1970).

————, 'The Galilean revolution: the historical fate of a methodological insight', *Studies in History and Philosophy of Science*, 2 (1972), 297–328.

Moyer, Donald F., 'Energy, dynamics, hidden machinery: Rankine, Thomson and Tait, Maxwell', *Studies in History and Philosophy of Science*, 8 (1977), 251–68.

Newton, Isaac, *Optice: sive de reflexionibus, refractionibus, inflexionibus & coloribus lucis*. Latine reddidit S. Clarke (London, 1706).

————, *Opticks: Or a Treatise of the Reflexions, Refractions, Inflexions and Colours of Light*, 4th ed., 1730 (reprinted, London, 1952).

————, *The Correspondence of Isaac Newton*, ed H. W. Turnbull, J. F. Scott, A. R. Hall and L. Tilling, 7 vols. (Cambridge, 1959–77).

————, *Unpublished Scientific Papers of Isaac Newton*, ed. A. R. Hall and M. Boas Hall (Cambridge, 1962).

————, *The Mathematical Papers of Isaac Newton*, ed. D. T. Whiteside, 8 vols. (Cambridge, 1967–81).

————, *Isaac Newton's Philosophiae Naturalis Principia Mathematica: The Third Edition (1726) with Variant Readings*, ed. A. Koyré and I. B. Cohen, 2 vols. (Cambridge/Cambridge, Mass., 1972).

Olson, Richard G., 'The reception of Boscovich's ideas in Scotland', *Isis*, 60 (1969), 91–103.

————, *Scottish Philosophy and British Physics 1750–1880. A Study in the Foundations of the Victorian Scientific Style* (Princeton, 1975).

Palter, Robert, 'Kant's formulation of the laws of motion', *Synthese*, 24 (1972), 96–116.

Paton, H. J., *Kant's Metaphysic of Experience*, 2 vols. (London, 1936).

Playfair, John, 'Biographical account of the late Dr James Hutton', *Transactions of the Royal Society of Edinburgh*, 5 (1805), 39–99.

————, *The Works of John Playfair*, 4 vols. (Edinburgh, 1822).

Poisson, Siméon Denis, 'Mémoire sur l'équilibre et le mouvement des corps élastiques', *Mémoires de l'Académie des Sciences*, 8 (1829), 357–570.

Polonoff, Irving I., *Force, Cosmos, Monads and Other Themes of Kant's Early Thought* (Bonn, 1973).

Priestley, F. E. L., 'The Clarke-Leibniz controversy', in *The Methodological Heritage of Newton*, ed. R. E. Butts and J. W. Davis (Oxford, 1970), pp. 34–56.

Priestley, Joseph, *Hartley's Theory of the Human Mind, on the Principle of the Association of Ideas; With Introductory Essays Relating to the Subject of It* (London, 1775).

————, *Disquisitions Relating to Matter and Spirit* (London, 1777); 2nd ed., 2 vols. (Birmingham, 1782).

————, *The Theological and Miscellaneous Works of Joseph Priestley*, ed. J. T. Rutt, 25 vols. (London, 1817–31).

Rankine, W. J. Macquorn, 'On the general law of the transformation of energy', *Philosophical Magazine*, 5 (1853), 106–17.

Reid, Thomas, *Essays on the Active Powers of the Human Mind*, ed. B. Brody (Cambridge, Mass., 1969).

Rowning, John, *A Compendious System of Natural Philosophy* (London, 1738–45).

Siegel, Daniel M., 'Thomson, Maxwell and the universal ether in Victorian physics', in *Conceptions of Ether*, ed. G. N. Cantor and M. J. S. Hodge (Cambridge, 1981), pp. 239–68.

Simpson, Thomas K., 'Some observations on Maxwell's *Treatise on Electricity and Magnetism*', *Studies in History and Philosophy of Science*, 1 (1970), 249–63.

Smith, Crosbie W., 'A new chart for British natural philosophy: the development of energy physics in the nineteenth century', *History of Science*, 16 (1978), 231–79.

Spencer, J. Brookes, 'Boscovich's theory and its relation to Faraday's researches: an analytic approach', *Archive for History of Exact Sciences*, 4 (1967), 184–202.

Stegmüller, Wolfgang, 'Towards a rational reconstruction of Kant's metaphysics of experience', *Ratio*, 9 (1967), 1–32; *ibid.*, 10 (1968), 1–37.

Thackray, Arnold, *Atoms and Powers: An Essay on Newtonian Matter–Theory and the Development of Chemistry* (Cambridge, Mass./Oxford, 1970).

Thomson, William, 'On the uniform motion of heat in homogeneous solid bodies, and its connection with the mathematical theory of electricity', *Cambridge Mathematical Journal*, 3 (1842), 71–84.

———, 'On a mechanical representation of electric, magnetic and galvanic forces', *Cambridge and Dublin Mathematical Journal*, 2 (1847), 61–4.

———, 'An account of Carnot's theory of the motive power of heat', *Transactions of the Royal Society of Edinburgh*, 16 (1849), 541–74.

———, 'On the dynamical theory of heat', *Transactions of the Royal Society of Edinburgh*, 4 (1851), 261–88.

———, 'On a universal tendency in nature to the dissipation of mechanical energy', *Philosophical Magazine*, 4 (1852), 304–6.

———, 'On the mechanical antecedents of motion, heat and light', *Report of the British Association (1854)* (London, 1855), part II, pp. 59–63.

———, 'Dynamical illustrations of the magnetic and heliocoidal rotary effects of transparent bodies on polarised light', *Proceedings of the Royal Society*, 8 (1856), 150–8.

———, *Mathematical and Physical Papers*, 6 vols. (Cambridge, 1882–1911).

Thomson, William and Tait, Peter Guthrie, *A Treatise on Natural Philosophy* (Oxford, 1867).

Timerding, H. E., 'Kant und Euler', *Kant-Studien*, 23 (1919), 18–64.

Torricelli, Evangelista, *Opere*, ed. G. Loria and G. Vassura, 4 vols. (Faenza, 1919–44).

Tuschling, Burkhard, *Metaphysische und transzendentale Dynamik in Kants opus postumum* (Berlin, 1971).

Tyndall, John and Francis, William, *Scientific Memoirs, Natural Philosophy* (London, 1853).

Vuillemin, Jules, *Physique et métaphysique Kantiennes* (Paris, 1955).

Walker, Adam, *A System of Familiar Philosophy*, 2nd ed., 2 vols. (London, 1802).

Werkmeister, W. H., 'The Critique of Pure Reason and physics', *Kant-Studien*, 68 (1977), 33–45.

Westfall, Richard S., *Force in Newton's Physics. The Science of Dynamics in the Seventeenth Century* (London/New York, 1971).

Whewell, William, *Philosophy of the Inductive Sciences, Founded upon their History*, 2nd ed., 2 vols. (London, 1847).

Whiteside, D. T., 'Before the *Principia*: the maturing of Newton's thought on dynamical astronomy, 1664–1684', *Journal for the History of Astronomy*, 1 (1970), 5–19.

———, 'The mathematical principles underlying Newton's *Principia Mathematica*', *Journal for the History of Astronomy*, 1 (1970), 116–38.

Williams, L. Pearce, *Michael Faraday: A Biography* (London, 1965).

Wise, M. Norton, 'German concepts of force, energy and the electromagnetic ether: 1845–1880', in *Conceptions of Ether*, ed. G. N. Cantor and M. J. S. Hodge (Cambridge, 1981), pp. 269–307.

Yolton, John W., *Locke and the Compass of Human Understanding* (Cambridge, 1970).

Index

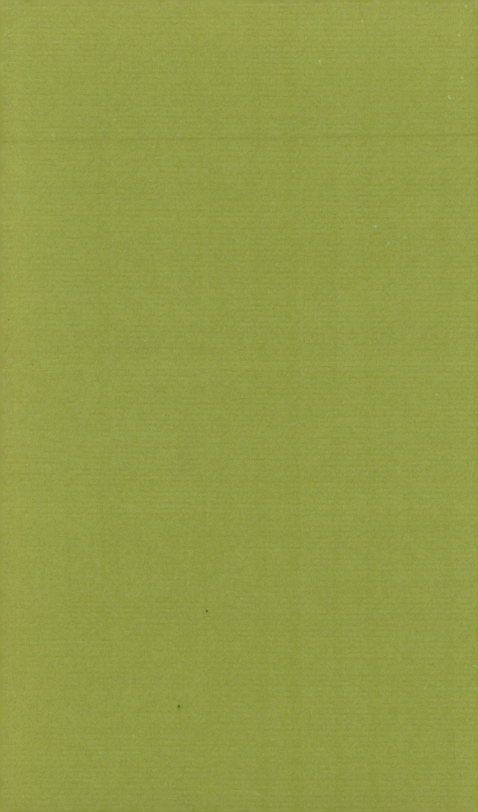